Oklahoma
THE LAND AND ITS PEOPLE

BY KENNY A. FRANKS AND PAUL F. LAMBERT

AMERICAN & WORLD GEOGRAPHIC PUBLISHING

Oklahoma Geographic Series NO. 1

ACKNOWLEDGMENTS

Much of the work in preserving Oklahoma's unique culture and heritage was done by Kent Ruth, Dr. John Morris, George Shirk, and Jim Argo, who for years traveled the highways and byways of Oklahoma searching out little known facets of the Sooner State. Their works, *Oklahoma Travel Handbook*, *Ghost Towns of Oklahoma*, and *Oklahoma: A Guide to the Sooner State*, take the reader off the beaten path and onto the colorful backroads of the state.

The two major sources of material on early Oklahoma history and geography are the Oklahoma Historical society, under the direction of Blake Wade and Dr. Bob Blackburn, and the Oklahoma Department of Libraries, headed by Robert Clark. Within the Oklahoma Historical Society are the invaluable collections held by the Indian Archives Division, headed by William D. Welge, and staff of Patsy Cooley and Rodger Harris. Among its holdings are thousands of historic photographs under the care of Chester R. Cowen. Researching this book would not have been possible without the help of a number of individuals at the Oklahoma Department of Libraries, including: Steve Beleu, William Boone, Chris Bitttle, Mike Cameron, Melecia Caruthers, Karen Fite, Carol Guilliams, Mary Harden, Virginia Martin, Betty Phillips, Kitty Pittman, and Mary Sweeney.

Of course, the invaluable editorial guidance offered by Teresa Record and staff of American & World Geographic Publishing did much to make this book a reality. We also appreciate the outstanding work of pioneer photographers, who captured the early-day history of Oklahoma, and their modern counterparts, whose works greatly enhance this book and provide a visual legacy of the Sooner State.

DEDICATION
This book is dedicated to the memory of
James Floyd Lambert.
A loving husband and devoted father,
he was a man of wisdom and integrity.

Library of Congress Cataloging-in-Publication Data
Franks, Kenny Arthur
    Oklahoma : the land and its people / by Kenny A. Franks and Paul F. Lambert.
        p.   cm. -- (Oklahoma geographic series; no. 1)
    Includes bibliographical references and index.
    ISBN 1-56037-044-0
    1. Oklahoma--Geography. I. Lambert, Paul F. II. Title.
III. Series.
F694.8.F7 1994
976.6--dc20   94-1554

Above: *The Tallgrass Prairie Preserve, with redbud trees.* JOHN ELK III

Title page: *The tranquil beauty of Oklahoma portrayed by the pool below Antelope Spring in the Chickasaw National Recreation Area.* LAURENCE PARENT

Front cover: *Seventy-seven-foot-tall Turner Falls on Honey Creek in the heart of the Arbuckle Mountains.* STEVE MULLIGAN

Back cover, top: *Kerr Park in downtown Oklahoma City.* JIM ARGO
Bottom: *Pawnee Indians dressed in ceremonial regalia for the annual Pawnee Indian Powwow.* JIM ARGO

HARVEY PAYNE

WARREN NEWELL

Above: *The fall foliage around Fort Gibson Lake in eastern Oklahoma attracts thousands of visitors annually.*
Top left: *The Tallgrass Prairie of Osage County is rich in wildlife, including this female cardinal.*

Facing page: *Native blue stem grass in the Tallgrass Prairie Preserve of Osage County.*

CONTENTS

HARVEY PAYNE

LAURENCE PARENT

Above: *Sunrise over the Charons Garden Wilderness in the Wichita Mountains National Wildlife Refuge of southwestern Oklahoma.*
Left: *A split-rail fence in picturesque eastern Oklahoma highlighted by Mexican Hat flowers.*

Facing page: *A spring thunderstorm over the rugged terrain of the Wichita Mountains.*

JOHN ELK III

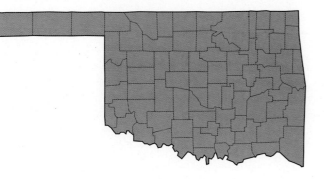

THE LAND

Oklahoma can be thought of as divided into two sections—the humid woodlands of the east and the semiarid grasslands of the west. This division is cultural as well as geographic. The eastern part of the state, with an annual rainfall of between 32 and 52 inches, resembles the timber covered hills and valleys of the South. Its climate provides sufficient rainfall for the growth of large stands of timber and such staples of Southern agriculture as corn and cotton. Populated first by Native Americans removed from the South and later by non-Indian settlers from Arkansas, East Texas and other Southern states, the area became a mirror of the Old South, with a distinct Southern culture complete with log cabins, split-rail fences and a subsistence agriculture.

The western portion of the state is drier, averaging between 16 and 30 inches of rain every year. Corn and cotton could not be grown prior to the extensive development of irrigation and there were insufficient trees to allow construction of log cabins or split-rail fences. Thus, Southern penetration of present-day Oklahoma was limited to east of the Cross Timbers, a dense impenetrable swath of scrub oak and blackjack trees.

It was at the Cross Timbers that the Wild West began. To its east, antebellum cotton plantations were established and a gentle Southern society developed. To its west were the nomadic Plains Indians following herds of buffalo. These warlike tribes discouraged early settlers from pushing west of the Cross Timbers. However, once the buffalo were slaughtered and the Plains Indians confined to reservations, this rich grassland attracted Texas stockmen. Moving onto the empty rangeland, they established vast herds of cattle. Thus western Oklahoma's culture developed more along the lines of the Old West, with widely spaced ranches interspersed with frontier communities.

The geographical formation of Oklahoma started 1.35 billion years ago, when ancient seas laid the foundation of the state's sedimentary rocks. Later, during the Cambrian Period, heat and fluids produced by molten matter beneath the earth's crust changed much of the older sedimentary rock into metamorphic rocks. At the same time, molten matter escaped to the surface solidified and formed igneous rocks. Oklahoma's topography was molded as portions of the state alternately were thrust upward or pulled downward by geological action. The sinking of the land below sea level created vast shallow seas that dominated the early Paleozoic Era. Afterward, a series of uplifts thrust the land above sea level. Where these upward thrusts occurred over broad areas, they formed gently rolling hills. More violent upthrusts caused extreme folding and faulting that created the state's three primary mountain belts—the Ouachitas, the Arbuckles and the Wichitas.

WARREN NEWELL

During the Cambrian, Ordovician, Silurian and Devonian periods, Oklahoma was covered by shallow seas. Thick deposits of limestone and dolomite were deposited. Later, during the Mississippian and Pennsylvanian periods, portions of the state sank more rapidly and more deeply than ever before and shale became intermingled with the beds of sandstone and limestone.

The Pennsylvanian Period was the era of great mountain-building in the state. The flat sedimentary rocks were uplifted drastically to form the Ouachita, Arbuckle and Wichita mountains. The Arbuckles, which are about 60 miles long and 20 miles wide, cover approximately 1,000 square miles in Carter, Murray, Pontotoc and Johnston counties, and are among the oldest mountains in America. The Ouachita Mountains cover LeFlore, McCurtain, Latimer, Pushmataha and Pittsburg counties, and eastward into Arkansas.

This violent period of mountain-building caused a drastic downthrust among the adjacent regions. Two huge basins, the Anadarko and Arkoma, and two lesser basins, the Hollis and the Ardmore, were created along the sides of the mountain chains. The Anadarko Basin underlies most of western Oklahoma south of the Canadian River and north of the Wichita Mountain Chain. The Arkoma Basin lies south of the Canadian River and north of the Arbuckle and Ouachita mountains. The Hollis Basin is south of the Wichitas and north of the Red River, and the Ardmore basin is south of the Arbuckle Mountains and north of the Gulf Coast Plain along the Red River.

Filling with water, these depressions formed shallow seas. These seas laid down thick layers of mud, sand and calcium skeletons of sea animals. Where rivers and streams emptied into the ancient seas, and along the shorelines and tidal inlets, additional alluvial and deltaic deposits were laid down. These deposits were buried, compressed and cemented together to form shale, sandstone and limestone. As the land sank

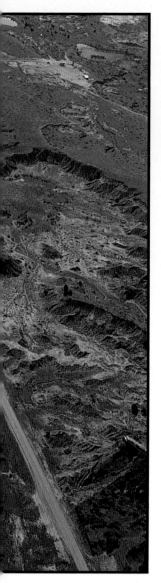

Facing page: Cathedral Mountain, a 300-foot tall crystalline butte in the Glass or Gloss Mountains west of Orienta in Major County, is a part of the Blaine Escarpment, a great gypsum formation stretching across much of western Oklahoma.

Left: Granite Mountain Quarry in the Quartz Mountains near Mangum. The 600- to 800-foot red granite hills attracted early-day Spanish miners searching for gold.

deeper, plants growing in the swamps and marshland along the edge of the ancient sea were buried to form the vast coal deposits in eastern Oklahoma.

Beginning during the Permian Era, most of western Oklahoma again was covered by a shallow sea. Erosion wore away the mountain chains. A warm dry climate resulted in the evaporation of much of the sea water, leaving behind huge deposits of gypsum and salt. These are most readily seen in the Great Salt Plains, Little Salt Plains and the Gypsum Hills of northwestern Oklahoma.

With the opening of the Tertiary Period, the land began a gradual rising above sea level. The ancient seas disappeared and the topography took on a gentle northwest-to-southeast slope in which the land drops from 5,000 feet above sea level near Black Mesa to 1,300 feet above sea level near Idabel. Volcanic activity increased.

As a result of the geological upheavals, Oklahoma developed a diverse topography, characterized by 26 geological configurations that vary from the Dissected Coastal Plain along the Red River to Black Mesa, a basaltic lava flow in the Panhandle. Southern Oklahoma's ancient mountain systems are characterized as the Arbuckle Hills and the Limestone Hills. Much of the state is covered with rolling hills, with steep bluffs and

caves that form the Arbuckle Hills, Arbuckle Plains, Arkansas Ridge and Valley Belt, Beavers Bend Hills, Boston Mountains, Cimarron Gypsum Hills, Granite Mountain Region, Hogback Frontal Belt, Limestone Hills, Mangum Gypsum Hills, McAlester Marginal Hills Belt, Ozark Plateau, Ridge and Valley Belt, Weatherford Gypsum Hills and Western Sandstone Hills. Others such as the Ardmore Basin and Neosho Lowland once were shallow seas. Much of the central and eastern part of the state is covered with cuestas, hills with a gentle slope on one side and a cliff on the other, overlooking shale, sandstone and limestone plains. These areas include the Northern Limestone Cuesta Plains, Central Redbed Plains, Claremore Cuesta Plains, Eastern Sandstone Cuesta Plains and the Western Redbed Plains. The Western Sand Dune Belt stretches along the rivers of western Oklahoma. The northwestern part of the state is characterized by the High Plains.

Oklahoma produced a variety of life during its period of prehistory. Among the oldest are the trilobites of the Cambrian Period. The Devonian Period was a time of huge carboniferous ferns and palm-like trees. The shallow swamps of the Panhandle during this period were the home of numerous carboniferous plants. Petrified logs, the fossilized remains of these carboniferous forest, have been found in Cimarron, Texas and Beaver counties. During the late Triassic Period, cycads—large palm-like trees topped with fern-like leaves and ornamented bark, and flowering gymno-

Left: Brontosaurus monument in Cimarron County, which contains one of the most prolific repositories of dinosaur fossils in the country.
Below left: Excavating dinosaur fossils north of Kenton in Cimarron County. Highway works building a roadway in 1931 first discovered the Panhandle's rich deposit of dinosaur fossils. The area has been excavated extensively since then and has contributed much to the understanding of the region's prehistory.

Facing page: The sun rising over the Wichita Mountains of southwestern Oklahoma. One of the most extensive mineralized areas in the Southwest, the Wichitas lured numerous early Spanish miners deep into their rugged interior.

sperms—with their cone-like fruit, were numerous. The rich, moisture-filled soil supported lush carpets of ferns and primitive flowering plants. Little grass covered the land, but in the higher elevations hardwood forest began to appear. The fossilized remains of a Shea oak, 3 feet in diameter and 15 feet in length, have been located in Beaver County. During some of this era, a part of the Oklahoma Panhandle was part of a vast inland Triassic Period sea.

The rich and abundant plant life and warm climate gave rise to numerous dinosaurs, making the Oklahoma Panhandle one of the most prolific areas of dinosaur fossils in the United States. In 1931 construction workers building US-64 through the region unearthed a myriad of dinosaur bones in Cimarron County near the Oklahoma-New Mexico border. In the following decades, numerous other dinosaur fossils and tracks have been located in the area around Kenton and on the Truman Tucker farm along the Oklahoma-Colorado border.

The fossils of several sauropods have been unearthed in southeastern Oklahoma and the Panhandle. Some were as small as 30 feet in length, while others, such as Brachiosaurus, Diplodocus and Brontosaurus or Apatosaurus, were huge, measuring as much as 100 feet from tail to head and weighing as much as 50 tons. In addition to their fossilized bones, the sauropods left behind deposits of gastroliths, or stomach stones. Other dinosaur fossils, including the bones of Acrocanthosaurus and Tenontosaurus, have been uncovered in southeastern Oklahoma.

The age of the dinosaurs ended with the Tertiary Period, and the age of mammals began. It was during this time that the Gulf of Mexico, which once extended into southeastern Oklahoma, began to recede, and the state's pattern of west-to-east flowing rivers developed. Following the Tertiary Period, the Quaternary Period was characterized by wide shifts in climate. Volcanoes were active in much of western and central Oklahoma during the Quaternary Period. Okfuskee County has some deposits of volcanic ash, and near Gate, in Beaver County, the ash is 40 feet deep.

The Quaternary Period is subdivided into the Pleistocene Epoch—the Great Ice Age—and the Holocene Epoch, or the modern era. At the onset of the Pleistocene Epoch the earth's temperature plunged. Much of the water solidified into huge glaciers, and the level of the seas fell as much as 300 feet. Although none of the huge sheets of ice reached Oklahoma, portions of the Panhandle and northeastern Oklahoma are covered by deposits of loess, which was formed when

the glaciers farther north ground rocks into powder that was blown south as dust and deposited as silt.

During the Holocene Epoch, Oklahoma's present climate and distribution of plants and animals began to occur. Swamps and lowlands were replaced by forest and then large expanses of grasslands. Mammals began to assert themselves, and the Great Plains was home to myriad now-extinct animals such as the ancestors to the modern buffalo, armadillo, llama, camel, hyena, tapir and mastodon. Later came the horse, mammoths and the American bison. Camel bones have been unearthed near Shattuck in Ellis County. Near Gate in the Oklahoma Panhandle the fossilized remains of a land tortoise, Geochelone, have been uncovered. Other tortoise remains have been found near Stecker in Caddo County in a prehistoric marsh, named the Domebo Site, that also contained the bones of ancient bog lemmings, muskrats, voles and cotton rats. The bones of a Columbian mammoth dated at over 17,000 years have been unearthed near Cooperton and Ketcher, while the fossilized remains of *Bison antiquus* have been found in what were the ancient marshlands.

Oklahoma contains some of the earliest indica-tions of human occupation on the continent. It was during the late Pleistocene Age that ancient people first wandered into Oklahoma. They were specialized hunters who had devised primitive tools. Some evidence indicates that the mammoth uncovered at Cooperton was killed by these primitive people who used stones to crush its bones. Undoubtedly, the Clovis Mammoth Hunters frequented this land, killing with shafts tipped with distinctive fluted projectile points. Downstream from the Domebo Site, Clovis points dating from approximately 11,200 years ago have been unearthed. Other finds near Anadarko and Frederick have produced stone tools dating from this period. Other Clovis points have been found in Cimarron and Tulsa counties. Numerous prehistoric human footprints also have been found in Cimarron County.

After the Clovis Mammoth Hunters came the Folsom Bison Hunters, who fed off of the huge prehistoric bison herds that roamed Oklahoma. Kill sites of those hunters also can be identified by distinctive projectile points. Folsom Points have been located in southwestern Cimarron, Caddo, Comanche, Marshall and Tulsa counties.

Right: *Entrance to a Pawnee earth lodge. The Pawnee were Prairie Indians and occupied the transition region of Oklahoma between the humid woodlands of the East and the arid prairie of the Great Plains.*

Facing page: *The pine-covered San Bois Mountains of southeastern Oklahoma are a part of the Ouachita Mountain chain that dominated the Choctaw Nation and divided the settlement of the area into a series of communities located in the valleys between the timber-covered ridges.*

After these ancient hunters came another series of people, who left more permanent indications in the rock ledges and caves of northeastern Oklahoma; the Panhandle; along the Red, Washita and Canadian rivers; near Mangum; and in southeastern Oklahoma. During their wanderings, these foragers habitually utilized the same campsites and water sources during the warmer months and the same ledges and caves during the colder months. In northeastern Oklahoma they were called the Ozark Bluff Dwellers, and in the Panhandle they were called the Basket Makers. These foragers flourished between 9,500 to 2,000 years ago.

Both they and other foragers had not yet developed the bow and arrow but hunted with throw sticks, called atlatl, that launched cane-shafted darts tipped with flint points. These were used to kill buffalo, deer, antelope and smaller game such as rabbits. These people also used curved nonreturnable boomerangs. Freshwater mussels also were part of their diet. Beside hunting tools they made crude but useful stone knives, scrapers, hammers and choppers from flint and fire drills of wood. They practiced rudimentary agriculture and ate wild seeds including acorns, and wild plums and berries. Before discovering how to fire pottery, they produced bark and fabric containers for storage, some lined with pitch as waterproofing. They lined pits with plants or stones for long-term storage of seeds and other food plants.

The Ozark Top-Layer Culture followed the earlier foragers. They also occupied the ledges and caves of northeastern Oklahoma, but they had developed the bow and arrow as an aid in hunting. They utilized fishing nets weighted with sinkers, and fishhooks. Animal bones, horns, and antlers became their agricultural implements, with corn one of their crops.

In the Panhandle, the Kenton Cave Dwellers, tentatively dated between 300 and 1500 C.E., flourished in a series of caves in northwestern Cimarron County. First uncovered in 1929, these caves have yielded a multitude of ancient artifacts, including red-tinted rock drawings, scratched-rock art and the naturally mummified remains of a young male child. An abundance of food has been identified in the caves, including cultivated corn and wild acorns, hackberries, cactus, sand plums and crocus bulbs. In addition, the bones of bison, deer, antelope, elk, rabbits, coyotes, wildcats, badgers, rodents, turtles, eagles and turkeys and the remains of fresh water mussels and crayfish were found. The Kenton Cave Dwellers utilized pottery, containers made of woven grass and skin, and ornamental shells.

About 2,000 years ago, Oklahoma's primitive people abandoned their cave and ledge dwellings and began constructing habitations. In eastern Oklahoma, the Mound Builders reached their cultural peak between 500 and 1500 C.E., and in the Panhandle the Slab-House culture flourished between 1000 and 1400 C.E. The Slab-House people dug pits, lined them with flat stones around the edge, emplaced central posts and used rafters to support reed and earth roofs. They made pottery, and lances and bows and arrows for weapons ,and they shaped stones into implements.

The Mound Builders constructed huge mounds that supported mud and wattle homes and served as religious shrines. Some of the mounds were solid.

Others were built over cedar frames and were hollow in the center. The tallest stood 40 feet in height. Advanced farmers, they tended crops of corn, beans, squash, pumpkins and sunflowers grown on river-bottom plots protected by levees. Of the several mound sites in southeastern Oklahoma, Spiro Mound and Williams Mound—both in LeFlore County—are the best known.

Excavation of the mounds has uncovered elaborate mazes of underground passageways and a multitude of artifacts including decorated pottery, cedar masks, rock-crystal carvings, beads, fiber baskets, animal furs and copper ear spools. The Mound Builders developed a complex society of workers, craftsmen, priests and warriors. Although war was an important part of their culture and the display of trophy heads a common ritual, they also developed an extensive trade network that brought goods from great distances. Just prior to the arrival of European explorers, however, the Mound Builders vanished.

At the time of the arrival of the European culture in Oklahoma, the land was claimed by several different tribes. One of the largest was the Wichita-Caddo Confederation. The Caddo established trade relations with the French as the latter arrived in Louisiana, and as a result of this contact soon were depleted by European diseases. By 1835 the Caddo were so reduced that the tribe was divided into three groups. One group migrated to the Hasinai Confederacy on the Brazos River in Texas, another group joined the Choctaw on the north side of the Red River in Oklahoma, and the third group joined The Bowl's group of Cherokees in Texas. The Wichitas also were forced from their homeland along the Red River and by the 1850s were concentrated around the Wichita Mountains and along Rush Creek in Grady County.

The Wichita-Caddo tribes were sedentary. They tilled the soil and built villages of elaborately covered conical thatched-grass lodges. Their diet included turtles, fish, shellfish and deer, as well as crops such as berries, nuts, corn, beans, sunflowers, pumpkins. They also grew tobacco. The men generally dressed in breechclouts of buckskin, moccasins, and fiber or cloth shirts.

Other indigenous Indian tribes in Oklahoma at the time of European exploration were the true Plains Indians. Nomadic and non-agricultural, these tribes had no permanent villages, but pursued the migrating herds of buffalo across the Great Plains. This group of Indians included portions of the Plains, or Kiowa-Apache, the Comanche, the Cheyenne and the Arapaho.

Their lifestyle was transformed dramatically with the arrival of the horse, reintroduced by the Spanish explorers. The horse gave them the mobility to follow the wandering herds of buffalo, and they created a

horse culture that presented early Europeans with a formidable foe. Armed with a small bow about three feet in length and made from ash, bois d'arc wood, or bone, a Plains Indian could drive an arrow through a buffalo. Plains Indians carried heavy shields of smoked buffalo hide that could turn a musket ball, and they could shoot arrows from a running horse so rapidly as to keep one or more arrows in the air at all times.

In north-central and northeastern portions of Oklahoma lived the Osage and Quapaw tribes, who were Prairie Indians. They occupied the region between the woodlands of the humid east and the plains of the arid west, and combined sedentary villages, with seasonal buffalo hunts onto the Great Plains.

Like the lifestyles of early tribes of Native Americans who occupied the region, Oklahoma's plant and animal kingdoms also reflected the state's two climatic zones: Eastern Oklahoma is predominantly timbered and covered with the same trees that characterize the Mississippi River Valley, and western Oklahoma is prairie, the trees concentrated along waterways, in species akin to those of the Great Plains. Because it occupies an area of transition between the hilly, forested East, and the flatter grasslands of the West, Oklahoma serves as an ecological borderland.

Oklahoma also is a cultural borderland. It occupies the region where the cultural East, West, Southwest and Midwest come together and, as the last part of the public domain opened to homesteaders, attracted a number of European immigrants. Because the settlement of the state took more than a century, from 1803 to 1907, Oklahoma was populated piecemeal and not in a systematic east to west migration. Aside from the indigenous Native Americans the modern settlement of

Oklahoma started with the removal of the Five Tribes—Choctaw, Creek, Cherokee, Chickasaw, and Seminole—in the 1820s. They populated the eastern half of the state. With the Reconstruction Treaties of 1866, their newly freed slaves formed a significant percentage of the region's population. Later, the northern section of eastern Oklahoma attracted a number of Eastern oilmen attracted by the rich oil and natural gas resources of the region. They gave northeastern Oklahoma a more Eastern outlook and cosmopolitan culture. Likewise, the southern portion of eastern Oklahoma became the home of a number of European nationalities attracted to the region's coal mining industry. They brought with them Old World traditions.

The western half was filled with Plains Indians beginning with the Medicine Lodge Treaty of 1867; however, they surrendered the land to two waves of homesteaders in the 1890s. The northern portion of western Oklahoma was settled in 1893 with the opening of the Cherokee Outlet. The people taking homesteads were predominately Northern, Midwestern or European farmers. The southern half had a more Western and Southwestern culture reflecting the early Spanish and Mexican penetration of the region and the cattle frontier.

The central core of Oklahoma—the Unassigned Lands—was opened to non-Indian settlement in 1889 and was populated by homesteaders from throughout the nation and several foreign countries. This gave this region a mixture of culture that differed from the other sections.

The Panhandle lived up to its name of "No Man's Land" and was the base of a Wild Western heritage reflecting its colorful legacy. Oklahoma's heritage reflects this bountiful cultural diversity. It truly is a "blending of many heritages."

Above: *Bare granite outcrops of the Wichita Mountains near Quanah Parker Lake in the Wichita Mountain Wildlife Refuge.*
Top: *Snow geese above the Sequoyah National Wildlife Refuge along the shore of Robert S. Kerr Lake in Eastern Oklahoma.*

Facing page: *Indian paintbrush covers a meadow among the blackjack and scrub-oak–covered terrain of Carter County, where wildcatters made one of the greatest oil discoveries in America.*

Above: *Hundreds of the best Native American dancers in the nation gather for Oklahoma City's annual Red Earth Festival.*

Top: *Dressed in tribal finery, a young contestant awaits his turn at the Red Earth Festival, an internationally recognized event held every spring in downtown Oklahoma City.*

Right: *Bill Mashunkashey, member of the Cherokee and the Osage tribes, on his land in Osage County.*

Facing page: *A nineteenth century Ponca Sun Dance on the Ponca Indian Reservation.*

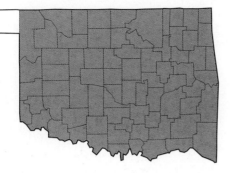

LAND OF THE RED PEOPLE

OKLA-HOMA

Oklahoma has an old and important cultural heritage inherited from Native Americans. This is reflected in the state's name, which is taken from the Choctaw words *Okla* meaning "people" and *Homa* meaning "red"—Red People. The state's Indian population is unique among the nation's Native Americans and is one of the largest concentrations of Native Americans in the country.

Although the present state of Oklahoma once was commonly known as Indian Territory, this is a misnomer. There was no officially created Indian Territory even though the Indian Removal Acts of 1830 and 1834 provided for the removal of Eastern Indians to a new home in the West. Instead, prior to the Civil War there were a series of independent/dependent Indian nations established in present-day Oklahoma—independent tribal governments insofar as the management of their internal affairs were concerned, but dependent upon the federal government for their existence. These tribes were mostly Eastern Indians removed to Oklahoma under the Indian Removal Act of 1830, or Prairie Indians who had lived in the region for centuries. Although the removal treaties granted these tribes all of present-day Oklahoma with the exception of the Panhandle, they remained concentrated in eastern Oklahoma in what at the time was called the Indian Nations.

Among them were the Five Tribes—the Choctaws, Creeks, Cherokees, Chickasaws, and Seminoles. The first of these Southeastern Indians to migrate to Oklahoma were the Choctaws. The Choctaws, who were spread throughout Louisiana, Alabama, and Mississippi, allied themselves with the Americans during the American Revolution. Afterward, the Treaty of Paris of 1783 and the Spanish-American Treaty of 1819 brought the Choctaws under the authority of the United States. In the 1820s, white settlers in the South began pressing for the removal of the Choctaws,

and under the provisions of the Treaty of Doaks Stand in 1825 and the Treaty of Dancing Rabbit Creek in 1830, the Choctaws exchanged their ancient homeland for a new land in southeastern Oklahoma. The tribe migrated westward between 1831 and 1834. In

ARCHIVES & MANUSCRIPT DIVISION OF THE OKLAHOMA HISTORICAL SOCIETY—DETAIL

1834, the Choctaws adopted a constitution and in 1838 a tribal capital was established at Nunih Waya, just west of present-day Tuskahoma. The Choctaw capital later was moved to Skullyville and then Doaksville. Present tribal headquarters is at Durant in Bryan County.

Closely related to the Choctaws were the Chickasaws who occupied portions of Mississippi and Alabama. As early as the 1700s, however, Chickasaw hunting and trading parties often visited Oklahoma. With the expansion of white settlers into the Old Southwest, the demand for the removal of the Chickasaws increased. Some Chickasaws began migrating to Oklahoma in the 1820s, and in 1832, the Chickasaws agreed to examine a potential homeland in the West; however, no specific agreement was reached until 1837 when the Treaty of Doaksville was signed. This agreement called for the division of the Choctaw Nation in Oklahoma into the Choctaw District and the Chickasaw District and gave the Chickasaws the same rights and privileges as the Choctaws. The land was held in common by the two tribes, but their finances were separate.

In 1855, the Chickasaws and Choctaws signed a treaty separating the two tribes, granting the Chickasaws ownership of the Chickasaw District, and selling the Leased District to the federal government. The Leased District included all lands held by the two tribes west of the 98th degree of longitude and was to be used as a permanent home for more peaceful Plains tribes. The current Chickasaw tribal headquarters is at Ada in Pontotoc County.

The Wichita and Caddo, who quickly were removed to the Leased District, were approximately 25 tribes formed into three confederations— the Kadohadocho, Hasinai, and Wichita. In 1835, the Caddo agreed to surrender their lands in Louisiana and move west where they divided into three groups: one joined the Hasinai Confederacy on the Brazos River in Texas; another group moved into the Choctaw Nation on the north side of the Red River; and the third party joined The Bowl's group of Cherokees in Texas. In 1858, the Caddo in Texas were moved to the Leased District where they settled along the Washita River. Binger in Caddo County is the current location of the Caddo tribal headquarters.

ROBERT C. GILDART

The Wichita migrated southward from Missouri under pressure from the Osage and Kaw, and settled along the Red River. By the 1850s the Wichita were concentrated around the Wichita Mountains of southwestern Oklahoma and along Rush Creek in Grady County. In 1859, the Wichita agreed to move to the Wichita Agency in the Leased District in what became the Wichita-Caddo Reservation. The tribe settled along the Caddo-Grady county line to the south of the Canadian River, and currently maintain its tribal headquarters at Anadarko in Caddo County.

The Wichita and Caddo soon were joined by other tribes expelled from the from the Brazos Reserve in Texas in 1859, and after the Civil War the tribes around the Wichita Agency were administered as the Wichita and Affiliated Tribes. Among them were the Anadarko, the Ioni (or Inie), the Kichai, and the Waco, which also were known as the Honeches, Huanchane, or Houechas.

The Cherokees were the next of the great Southeastern tribes affected by the Indian removal policy; however, their migration to Oklahoma was spread over several decades as three distinct groups migrated at different times. In 1777, a band of Cherokees under Dragging Canoe settled near present-day Chattanooga, Tennessee. They became known as the Chickamaugas. In 1794, under the leadership of The Bowl, they moved west into Arkansas and Texas. Those in Arkansas often traveled westward into present-day Oklahoma in search of buffalo, and in 1828 they exchanged their Arkansas homeland for land in northwestern Oklahoma and a perpetual outlet to their western hunting grounds, the Cherokee Outlet. Here they established the Cherokee Nation, West and became known as the Old Settlers.

The main body of Cherokees, the Cherokee Nation, East, remained in Georgia until the discovery of gold in 1830 led to a demand for their removal. A minority group, known as the Treaty Party, signed the Treaty of New Echota in 1835 committing the tribe to a new home in Oklahoma. These Cherokees moved west in 1835 and 1836 with little difficulty and joined the Old Settlers in the Cherokee Nation, West; however, the majority of the tribe, the Anti-Treaty Party, under principal chief John Ross, resisted. Eventually they were herded westward over the infamous Trail of Tears. Approximately 25 percent died during the journey. In 1839 the Old Settlers, the Treaty Party, and the Anti-Treaty Party were

Above: A typical Plains Indian teepee.
Top: A Cherokee woman weaving a grass basket at Tsa-La-Gi. The goal of the Cherokee Heritage Center is to preserve such tribal crafts.

Facing page: A young Cherokee boy at the Cherokee Heritage Center at Tsa-La-Gi near Tahlequah.

reunited by the Cherokee Act of Union in 1839, and the tribal capital was established at Tahlequah in Cherokee County.

One of the most recent Native American tribes to be recognized by the federal government is the United Keetoowah, which originally were part of the Cherokee Nation. Their tribal headquarters also is located in Tahlequah.

The Muscogee (or Muskogee) Confederation is composed of the Alabama, Koasati, Hitchiti, Natchez, Yuchi, Tuskegee, and some Shawnee, but is dominated by the Creeks. The confederacy is commonly called Creeks, after the Ochese Creek Indians, a name given the tribe by early British traders. The Creeks themselves are divided into the Upper Creek, who originally lived along the Coosa and Tallapoosa rivers in Alabama and Georgia, and the Lower Creeks, who lived along the Chattahooche and Flint rivers near the Alabama-Georgia border. Each band in the Creek Confederacy had its own town.

The Creeks often were at war with non-Indian settlers. The Red Sticks, the Upper Creeks, and many of the Lower Creeks joined in Tecumseh's Rebellion during the War of 1812, and were defeated at the Battle of Horseshoe Bend in 1814. Pushed to move west, the Creeks divided over the issue and in 1824 a blood law was passed providing for the death penalty for ceding tribal lands. Nonetheless, a treaty was signed with one tribal faction the following year providing for removal to the west. The leader of this minority faction, William McIntosh, was killed according to the blood law. In 1826, however, another removal treaty was signed with the McIntosh party, and beginning in 1828 some Creeks began migrating to their new home in Oklahoma. In 1832 a final removal treaty was signed and those Creeks remaining in Alabama were to move west within five years. The result was the Creek War of 1835-1836 and the forcible removal of the tribe by the military.

The Upper and Lower Creeks were reunited as the Creek Nation, West in 1839, but the tribe remained split along the old division. The Upper Creeks settled along the North Canadian and Deep Fork of the Canadian rivers, while the Lower Creeks settled along the Arkansas River between the Verdigris and Red Fork rivers. In addition, the concept of the Creek Confederacy was maintained with several affiliated bands welcomed into the Creek Nation, West, and for a short period the Seminoles were settled among the Creeks. By 1856, there were also bands of Shawnee, Delaware, Quapaw, Kickapoo, and Piankashaw living within the Creek Nation. The capital of the Muscogee Nation is Okmulgee in Okmulgee County.

Among the other tribes that migrated with the Five

Tribes were the Natchez, who lived along the lower Mississippi River. The Natchez virtually were destroyed by the French in 1729, and those who survived sought refuge among the Chickasaws, Cherokees, and Creeks. Intermarriage with these tribes destroyed the true Natchez bloodline; however, many mixed-blood Natchez-Chickasaws, Natchez-Cherokees, and Natchez-Creeks were removed to present-day Oklahoma.

The Catawba and the Iswa were from South Carolina. In 1851 they began migrating to Indian Territory and settled among the Five Tribes. Most of the Catawbas and Iswas settled along the Canadian River between the Choctaw and Creek nations. The Koasati or Quassarte, had joined the Muscogee Confederacy in the late 1600s and were removed to the Creek Nation in 1836.

The Tuskegee divided into two groups: one joined the Cherokees and the other joined the Muscogee Confederacy. Both groups were removed to Indian Territory with the Cherokees and Creeks. The Yuchi, or Euchee or Uchee, who had joined the Lower Creeks also were removed to Indian Territory with the Creeks. In 1867 the Yuchi were made a part of the Muscogee Nation and given representation in the National Council.

The last of the large Eastern tribes removed to Oklahoma were the Seminoles, who once were a part of the Muscogee Nation driven out of Georgia, and Oconee and Yamasee tribes driven out of the Carolinas to settle in Spanish Florida. They were joined by other Creeks following the Red Stick War of 1813-1814 and fugitive slaves fleeing to Florida and freedom. They became known as *Semino'le,* the Creek word for "run away."

Top: A portion of the black students enrolled in the Creek-Seminole College at Boley. Before their removal to Indian Territory, the Seminoles offered a haven for runaway slaves who would flee to their Florida homeland. These blacks were accepted into the tribe and became an integral part of the Seminole Nation. Boley once was touted as the largest all-black community in the United States.

Left: The log cabin that served as the Seminole Nation Council House following the Civil War.

In 1819, Spain ceded Florida to the United States and brought the Seminoles under American jurisdiction. Almost immediately the Americans demanded the return of any runaway slaves and the removal of the Seminoles from the rich Florida farmland. In 1823, the Seminoles were granted a tract of land in the Everglades. The Seminoles found it difficult to survive in the swamp and slave hunters constantly kidnapped black members of the tribe and returned them to Georgia as slaves. In 1832 the Treaty of Payne's Landing provided for the removal of the Seminoles to the Creek Nation in Indian Territory. An exploring party visited Indian Territory and signed another treaty at Fort Gibson in 1833 calling for the merger with the Creek Nation.

When the delegation returned to Florida, however, they found that most Seminoles opposed the merger and renounced both the Treaty of Fort Gibson and the Treaty of Payne's Landing. Nonetheless, federal officials insisted that Seminoles move west, and when troops were sent into the Everglades, the first of three Seminole Wars broke out. These proved to be the largest and most expensive of all Indian wars fought by the United States and it was not until 1858 that the last Seminole was removed to Indian Territory.

Most settled between the Canadian and North Canadian rivers in the western part of the Creek Nation. However, disputes between the Creeks and Seminoles resulted in an 1845 agreement that allowed the Seminoles to settle as a body, maintain their own tribal government, and enforce Seminole laws. In 1856, the Seminoles and Creeks were divided and the Seminoles were granted their own nation in the western part of the Creek Nation. Their national capital is maintained at Wewoka in Seminole County.

During the Civil War the Five Tribes split in their allegiance, with the majority of the Choctaws and Chickasaws joining the South and the Cherokee, Creeks, and Seminoles dividing almost evenly between loyalty to the North and joining the Southern Confederacy. Following the fight, however, no matter their allegiance, all members of the tribes were treated as allies of the South and in a series of reconstruction treaties stripped of their lands in the western one-half of the state. It was on this newly acquired territory that the federal government planned to create reservations for the Plains Indians. These became reservations in the total meaning of the word, complete with federally appointed agents controlling the day-to-day existence of the tribes and with little official tribal autonomy.

The first settlement of Plains Indians on permanent reserves in Oklahoma was made under the provisions of the Treaties of Medicine Lodge signed in 1867 by the Kiowas, Comanches, Cheyenne, Arapaho, and Prairie Apaches. The Kiowa and Comanches were the first to yield to the insistence of the federal government to abandon their nomadic lifestyle and signed the treaty on October 18, 1867. The Comanches are divided into 12 different bands, but the two bands most prominent in Oklahoma's history are the *Penateka*, or "honey eaters," and the *Kwahari*, or "antelopes." Their first contact with the United States came in 1834 when they met with the Dragoon Expedition in Kiowa County and the following year a portion of the tribe signed the Treaty of Camp Holmes. Typical Plains Indians, the Kiowa and Comanches were allies and often were called the Kiowa-Comanches. The Medicine Lodge Treaty assigned them a reservation between the Canadian and Red rivers west of the 98th Meridian and provided that the reservation was to be shared with the Prairie Apaches, also called the Kiowa-Apaches, who signed the treaty on October 21, 1867. The Comanches' tribal headquarters is at Lawton in Comanche County, while the Kiowa maintain their tribal headquarters at Carnegie in Caddo County and Apache headquarters is at Anadarko in Caddo County.

Joining them were portions of the Lipan Apache. Originally living on the Southern Plains, the Lipan were pushed south into Texas and Mexico by the Comanche. In 1846, the some of the Texas Lipan were settled on the Brazos Reservation, and in 1859 this group was removed to the Wichita Agency in Indian Territory. Most of these Lipan merged with the Kiowa-Apache in 1895 and settled on the Kiowa-Comanche-Apache Reservation. Another group of Texas Lipan joined with the Tonkawa and in 1885, this band was removed to Indian Territory with the Tonkawa and settled on the former Nez Perce reservation in Kay County.

The Fort Sill Apache, also called the Chiricahua, Warm Springs, Wild, or Eastern Apache also settled on the Comanche-Kiowa-Apache Reservation. They were true buffalo Indians, who had been defeated by the Comanches and driven off the Great Plains into west Texas, Arizona, and New Mexico. By 1873, most of the Chiricahuas were settled on the Chiricahua Reservation in southeastern Arizona, but in 1875 they were moved to the San Carlos Reservation alongside the Warm Spring and other Apache bands. Led by Victorio, Nana, Geronimo, and others, portions of the Chiricahua and Warm Springs bands broke out, and intermittent warfare continued until 1886, when Geronimo was captured. Sent first to Florida and then Alabama, the Chiricahua and Warm Springs Apaches finally were settled around Fort Sill in 1894. They remained at Fort Sill as prisoners of war until 1913, when they were given the choice of remaining in Oklahoma or moving to New Mexico. Eighty-seven remained near Fort Sill and purchased 80 acre homesteads from the Kiowa-Comanches. Their tribal headquarters is at Apache in Caddo County.

The Cheyenne-Arapho were the other Great

Plains tribe that signed a treaty at Medicine Lodge. Around 1835 the Arapaho separated into two distinct bands—the Northern Arapaho and the Southern Arapaho. The Northern Arapaho settled in Wyoming and Montana and the Southern Arapaho settled along the Arkansas River in Colorado, Kansas, and Oklahoma. The Southern Arapaho were typical horse Indians. In 1861, the Southern Arapaho signed a treaty at Fort Wise, Kansas, and joined with the Southern Cheyenne tribe. Since then they have been known as the Cheyenne-Arapaho.

The Cheyenne, who also were horse Indians, signed a treaty with the federal government in 1825, and shortly afterward the tribe split into two factions—the Southern Cheyenne and the Northern Cheyenne. The Northern Cheyenne moved northward and settled along the Platte and Yellowstone rivers in Montana and Wyoming. The Southern Cheyenne settled along the Arkansas River in Colorado, Kansas, and Oklahoma.

The Southern Cheyenne signed the Treaty of Medicine Lodge on October 28, 1867; however, it was not until August 10, 1869 that the boundary of the Cheyenne-Arapaho Reservation was established permanently

as south of the Cherokee Outlet along the North Fork of the Canadian River. The Cheyenne-Arapaho were served by the Darlington Agency, near El Reno in Canadian County. Their current tribal headquarters is at Concho in Canadian County.

By the 1870s Oklahoma had become the primary location for the resettlement of Native Americans from throughout the country and thousands of Indians were forced to accept new homes in the region. Among them were the Delaware, who were divided into three tribal bands—the Minsi, Unami, and Unalachitigo. Originally from New York, Pennsylvania, and New Jersey, the Delaware were pushed westward by colonists first to Ohio and then in 1782 most continued west across the Mississippi River. As early as 1812 the Delaware began hunting in what became Oklahoma, and by 1839 so many lived in the northeastern portion of the Cherokee Nation that the Delaware District was created from all or parts of Craig, Mayes, Delaware, and Ottawa counties. These became known as the Registered Delaware; an 1867 agreement paid the Cherokee $1 an acre for 157,000 acres in Washington County. The agreement also gave the Registered Dela-

Above: Drum players providing music for tribal dances at the Pawnee Memorial Day Pow Wow in Pawnee.

Right: A Southern Ute war dancer performing at a Native American ceremonial dance contest in Norman. The state's internationally acclaimed Indian dance contests regularly attract contestants from tribes throughout the nation.

Facing page: Kiowa flute player, Tom Ware, performing at Indian City, USA near Anadarko.

ware equal right and equal participation in the Cherokee tribal government and tribal revenues.

In 1830, those Delaware who had remained in Indiana, Ohio, and Missouri accepted a new reservation in Kansas. In 1866, a treaty was signed allowing the Delaware in Kansas either to become citizens of the United States and remain in Kansas or to retain their tribal affiliation and join their fellow tribesmen in the Cherokee Nation. The Registered Delaware maintain their tribal headquarters in Bartlesville in Washington County.

The Registered Delaware were joined by the Munsee or Christian Indians, who once had been a part of the Delaware tribe, but during the War of 1812 had fled to Canada and joined with the Chippewa. In 1832, a band of Munsee joined with the Stockbridge Indians on a reservation near Winnebago Lake, Wisconsin. Thereafter, both bands were known as the Munsee or Christian Indians. In 1839, 169 Munsee emigrated to the Delaware Reservation in Kansas. In 1867, they joined the Delaware in moving to the Cherokee Nation.

The Delaware of Western Oklahoma are portions of the Delaware tribe that migrated southwest from their homeland and joined the Caddo and Wichita tribes in Texas. In 1858 they were assigned a home on the Lower Reserve along the Brazos River in Texas. Later that same year they were moved to the Wichita Agency in the Leased District. Their tribal headquarters is in Anadarko.

Close behind the Delaware came the Shawnee, once one of the most powerful tribes in the Ohio River Valley. The warlike Shawnee were defeated in the French and Indian War, Pontiac's Rebellion, the Revolutionary War, and Tecumseh's Revolt. This series of wars destroyed the tribe and divided it into several groups. Some remained in Ohio, but most moved westward. The Absentee-Shawnee migrated into the Creek and Choctaw nations or joined the Texas Cherokee. Some of the Ohio Shawnee joined with the Seneca and later settled in Ottawa County. This group was known as the Eastern Shawnee.

Others, who were called the Shawnee of Missouri or Black Bob's Shawnee settled in Kansas. In 1871 Shawnee of Missouri accepted new homes in the northern part of the Cherokee Nation. As part of the agreement they were admitted to the Cherokee tribe. They maintained a Shawnee Business Committee headquartered in Vinita until the allotment of the Cherokee lands and the abolition of tribal governments. Currently they are organized as the Cherokee-Shawnee and maintain their tribal headquarters at Miami.

The Absentee-Shawnee moved south and west with some settling in the Choctaw and Creek nations, while others continued into Louisiana and Texas. In 1839, those Shawnee who had settled in Texas were driven out and forced to seek refuge with the Eastern Shawnee in the Cherokee Nation. During the general Indian expulsion from Texas in 1859 another band of Texas Shawnee were removed to the Wichita Agency in Caddo County; they became known as the Absentee-Shawnee.

In 1867 an agreement was reached allowing the Absentee-Shawnee at the Wichita Agency to be resettled in the Seminole Nation. Although the treaty was not ratified by the federal government, many of the members of this band moved to present-day Cleveland, Oklahoma, and Pottawatomie counties on land reserved for the Potawatomi. They were served by the Sac and Fox Agency near Stroud. In was not until 1872 that the move officially was sanctioned by federal officials. They maintain their tribal headquarters at Shawnee in Pottawatomie County.

The Citizen Band of Potawatomi originated around the upper reaches of Lake Huron, but moved into Illinois and Indiana. In treaties signed in 1833 and 1837 they ceded most of their homeland and the majority of the Potawatomi moved west of the Mississippi River. Two distinct bands developed: the Prairie Potawatomi, who settled in Iowa, and the Potawatomi of the Woods, who settled in Kansas. In 1846, the Prairie Potawatomi, Potawatomi of the Woods, Ojibway, and Ottawa were placed on a reservation in Kansas, but pressure from settlers lead to another treaty in 1861 that offered individual allotments and American citizenship.

The Potawatomi of the Woods accepted the allotments and became citizens of the United States. Henceforth they were known as the Citizen Band of Potawatomi. The Prairie Potawatomi refused the allotment and were placed on a 11-square-mile reserve in Kansas. In 1867 the Citizen Band of Potawatomi negotiated an agreement that granted the tribe a 30-square mile reservation in Indian Territory, which covered most of Pottawatomie and the extreme eastern parts of Oklahoma and Cleveland counties. They shared the reservation with the Absentee-Shawnee. Their tribal headquarters is in Shawnee.

The Osage once included what later became the Quapaw, Omaha, Ponca, and Kaw who divided into individual tribes during a long period of migration from the Midwest to the Atlantic Coast and back. When the tribe arrived at the Mississippi River, the Kaw moved downstream to the Arkansas River; the Omaha, Ponca, and Kaw moved upstream to the Missouri River; and the Osage remained on the Osage River in Missouri. The Osage themselves divided into the Little Osage and the Great Osage.

Between 1808 and 1825, the Osage ceded their homeland and accepted a reservation in Kansas. During the Civil War, members of the Great Osage enlisted in the Confederate army and fought as the Osage

Battalion, while members of the Little Osage fought for the North. At the end of the war, the Osages were forced to cede much of their land in Kansas as punishment for the actions of the Great Osage. In 1870 the Osage sold their land in Kansas and purchased a new reservation in Indian Territory, present-day Osage County. By 1872 the Osage were settled in their new home and in 1881 the Osage Nation was established, with its capital at Pawhuska in Osage County.

The Kaw or Kansa settled in Nebraska and Kansas. Beginning in 1820 they relinquished their homeland under a series of treaties, which ended in 1846 when they were moved to a 20-square-mile reservation in

and remove to Indian Territory. The tribe selected an area in present-day Pawnee and Payne counties. The sale was completed in 1876 and the Pawnee moved to their new land. A Pawnee Subagency was maintained on Black Bear Creek, and later a tribal headquarters was opened at Pawnee in Pawnee County.

The Ponca settled in southwest Minnesota and the Black Hills of South Dakota and later were joined by the Omaha. In 1858, the Ponca were assigned a reservation along the Niobrara River in Nebraska and ceded the remainder of their lands to the United States. In 1865, two-thirds of their Niobrara reservation was ceded, and in 1876 congress ordered the Ponca re-

Kansas. In 1872, the Kaw sold this reservation to the federal government and a new reserve was purchased from the Osage in Kay County, Oklahoma, where they were served by the Kaw Subagency of the Osage Agency. Later a tribal headquarters was opened at Kaw City in Kay County.

The Pawnee are divided into four confederated bands and two major groups, the Southern or Black Pawnee and the Skidi Pawnee. The Southern Pawnee originally ranged from the Rio Grande to the Arkansas River, with the Skidi Pawnee settled along the Platte, Loup, and Republican rivers in Nebraska. In the later part of the eighteenth century the two groups reunited in Nebraska. In a series of treaties in 1833, 1848, and 1857, the Pawnee surrendered their homeland for a reservation along the Loup River in Nebraska. In 1872, the Pawnee agreed to sell their Nebraska reservation

Often described as a mile wide and a foot deep, the Canadian River marked the boundary between the Choctaw and Chickasaw nations on the south and the Cherokee, Creek, and Seminole nations on the north.

Above: *Oklahoma is the home of many major Native American artists. This mural in Hominy was painted by Cha Tullis.*
Right: *One of the best known figures of Native American history was George Guess, or Sequoyah, the inventor of the Cherokee alphabet. Standing before his restored home near Sallisaw is this statue dedicated to his achievements.*

Facing page: *The historic Cherokee Female Seminary, now a part of the campus of Northeastern Oklahoma State University in Tahlequah.*

moved to Indian Territory. Troops were used to force the migration to the Quapaw Agency in Ottawa County in 1877. Later the tribe was moved to another reservation along the Salt Fork River in Kay and Noble counties and opened a tribal headquarters at Ponca City in Kay County.

The Nez Perce lived on a reservation in Oregon's Wallowa Valley and along Idaho's Salmon River. In 1863, after gold had been found in the Wallowa Mountains, federal officials began pressuring the Nez Perce to surrender their land and move to the Lapwai Reservation in Idaho. The Nez Perce refused and in 1875 federal officials declared the Wallowa Valley open to homesteaders. Fighting broke out, and Chief Joseph of the Nez Perce decided to take his tribe to Canada. Thus began a 1,700-mile flight of about 750 Nez Perce. Pursued by the military, the Indians were within 40 miles of Canada when they were defeated in the Bears Paw Mountains on September 30, 1877. At first the Nez Perce were sent to Kansas, and then in 1879 were settled on a reservation along the Chikaskia River in southwestern Kay County. In 1885, they were allowed to return to the Pacific Northwest and their land was given to the Tonkawa.

The Otoe and Missouria are two bands of the same tribe that originated around the Great Lakes be-fore migrating southwest in search of buffalo; they settled at the mouth of the Grand River. Here the tribe split with those moving upstream becoming the Otoe and those remaining behind becoming the Missouria. Between 1817 and 1841 the Otoe lived around the mouth of the Platte River in Nebraska, and in 1829 they were rejoined by the Missouria. In 1854, the Otoe-Missouira ceded their land around the Platte for a reservation along the Big Blue River on the Kansas-Nebraska border. In 1881, this reservation was sold and the Otoe-Missouria purchased a new reservation from the Cherokees in the Cherokee Outlet in Noble and Pawnee counties. By 1883 most tribal members had been relocated. Their tribal headquarters is at Red Rock in Noble County.

The Kickapoo, also known as the Mexican Kick-apoo and the Texas Kickapoo, are closely related to the Sac and Fox. Originally from southern Wisconsin, the Kickapoo moved southward into Illinois and set-tled along the Wabash River. Between 1809 and 1819, the Kickapoo sold their land in Illinois and migrated westward to Missouri. In 1832, they were assigned a 12-square-mile reservation in northeastern Kansas along the Missouri River.

In 1819, a portion of the tribe moved to Texas and joined the Texas Cherokees. In 1839, these Texas

Kickapoos were driven out of Texas and settled along Wild Horse Creek in the Choctaw Nation, in Garvin County. Another band of Texas Kickapoo settled along the Canadian River in the Creek Nation near the mouth of Little River. In 1852, a portion of the Kansas Kickapoo Reservaton was opened to homesteaders, and those who became known as the Mexican Kickapoo joined with a band of Potawatomi and moved first to Texas and later to Mexico. During the Civil War, in 1863, the Texas Kickapoo of the Creek Nation also moved south to join the Mexican Kickapoo.

In 1870, federal agents attempted to convince the Mexican Kickapoo to return to the United States, and in 1873 a portion of the tribe agreed. Those who remained in Mexico were given a reservation along the Sabinas River in Coahuila. In 1883, the Kickapoo were given a reservation west of the Sac and Fox Reservation along the Deep Fork of the Canadian in Oklahoma, Pottawatomie, and Lincoln counties. Tribal headquarters is at McLoud.

The Iowa are related closely to the Winnebago. They migrated to Minnesota from north of the Great Lakes. Later they migrated to the shore of the Missouri River near Council Bluffs, Iowa, and then to the region near the Des Moines River in Iowa and the Grand and Platte rivers in Missouri. In 1836 the Iowa accepted a 400-square-mile reservation with the Sac and Fox of the Missouri along the Great Nemaha River in Iowa.

In 1876 the tribe split, with one group moving to the Sac and Fox Reservation in Indian Territory and the other to Kansas. In 1883, the federal government granted the Iowa a reservation west of the Sac and Fox between the Cimarron and Deep Fork of the Canadian rivers in parts of Payne, Logan, Oklahoma and Lincoln counties. Tribal headquarters is in Perkins.

The Tonkawa originally were from the Trinity River area of Texas but moved southwest along the Texas-Mexican border. In 1855, the Tonkawa were settled on the Lower Reserve along the Brazos River in Texas with the Caddo and Anadarko. In 1859, the Tonkawa were removed to the Leased District and placed under the supervision of the Wichita Agency. During the Civil War the Tonkawa fought as allies of the Confederacy, and on October 22, 1862, an attack on their village by a force of Delaware and Shawnee armed by federal officials practically destroyed the tribe. The few Tonkawa who survived fled to Fort Arbuckle and remained refugees in the Chickasaw Nation until the war was over, when they were concentrated near Fort Griffin, Texas. In 1885, the Tonkawa were settled on the old Nez Perce reserve in Kay County. Tribal headquarters is in Tonkawa.

The Sac or Sauk and Fox were originally two independent—but closely related—tribes who lived around the Great Lakes. When the Chippewa encroached onto their tribal lands, the Sac and Fox formed an alliance.

Pushed west, the tribes split, with most Sac and Fox settling along the Des Moines River in Iowa and Illinois, and smaller groups settling along the Mississippi River, and the Missouri and Osage rivers in Missouri. These became known as the Sac and Fox of the Mississippi and the Missouri Sac and Fox.

Under pressure to remove west, the Sac and Fox east of the Mississippi rebelled in the Black Hawk War. Defeated, the Sac and Fox signed the Treaty of Fort Armstrong in 1832, which pushed the tribe out of Illinois and into Iowa. In 1845 and 1846 the Sac and Fox remaining in Iowa were moved west and joined with the Sac and Fox of the Mississippi. Through a series of treaties signed in 1842, 1854, 1859, and 1861, the Sac and Fox of Missouri were settled on a reservation in Doniphan County, Kansas, and the Sac and Fox of Mississippi on a reservation in Osage County, Kansas.

In 1867 the Sac and Fox of the Mississippi sold their land in Kansas and accepted a reservation in Indian Territory, in Lincoln, Payne, and Pottawatomie counties. In 1885, they organized the Sac and Fox Nation. In 1886, the remaining Sac and Fox were brought to Indian Territory. Tribal headquarters is in Stroud.

During the period of Indian removal to Oklahoma, other tribes were concentrated in the extreme northeastern portion of the state on land purchased from the Cherokee Nation. Among them were the Seneca-Cayuga, a confederation of Iroquois that included the Mingoes, Conestoga, Cayuga, Mohawk, Erie, Oneida, Tuscarora, Onondaga, Seneca of Sandusky, and Shawnee of Ohio. Their tribal domain stretched throughout the Old Northwest Territory. In 1817, the Senca of Sandusky accepted a reservation in Ohio along the Sandusky River, where they were joined by the Shawnee of Ohio and the other members of the Seneca-Cayuga confederacy. In 1831, the Seneca-Cayuga sold their land in Ohio and accepted a reservation in the Cherokee Nation and settled in present-day Delaware and Ottawa counties.

In 1867 the Omnibus Treaty sold part of the Seneca-Cayuga lands to the Wyandotte, Ottawa, Peoria, Kaskaskia, Wea, Piankashaw, and other affiliated tribes and provided for the separation of the Shawnee, who henceforth were known as the Eastern Shawnee, from the Seneca-Cayuga. In 1881, a band of Cayuga from Canada joined the Seneca-Cayuga in Indian Territory. Tribal headquarters is in Miami.

Originally from Canada, the Wyandotte moved west, eventually settling in Michigan, Ohio, and Indiana. In 1815, they were given a large tract of land in Ohio and Michigan for their support of the United States in the War of 1812. Beginning in 1795 and ending in 1842, the Wyandotte ceded their lands east of the Mississippi River and accepted a reservation at the junction of the Kansas and Missouri rivers in Wyandotte County, Kansas. In 1855, they were made citizens of the United States and given individual allotments; however, a portion of the tribe chose to move to Indian Territory where they purchased 33,000 acres from the Seneca in Ottawa County. During the Civil War they fled to Kansas, and as a result of the Omnibus Treaty of 1865 the Wyandotte were given a 20,000-acre reservation in Ottawa County. In 1871, most of the Wyandotte who had remained in Kansas joined those already in Indian Territory. They were managed by the Quapaw Agency and currently maintain their tribal headquarters at Wyandotte in Ottawa County.

The Eastern Shawnee originally were a part of the Shawnee living in South Carolina, Georgia, Tennessee, Pennsylvania, and Ohio. Forced westward, they broke into several bands, settling in Kansas, Texas, Louisiana, and Indian Territory. In 1832, a group of Shawnee who had remained behind in Ohio joined with the Seneca-Cayuga. Known as the Mixed Shawnee, they later were named the Eastern Shawnee. The Mixed Shawnee shared the fate of the Seneca and were moved westward with them. In 1867 they accepted a reservation the present-day Ottawa County, where they were served by the Quapaw Agency in Miami. Tribal headquarters in Quapaw.

The Ottawa also were removed to northeastern Oklahoma. Originally from Canada, they were driven south by the Iroquois and settled around the Great Lakes and in northern Illinois. In 1833, one band of Ottawa accepted a reservation in Franklin County, Kansas. In 1862, the Kansas band of Ottawa signed another treaty, which allotted their Kansas lands and sold the rest to homesteaders. Under the agreement the Ottawa tribal council was to be dissolved within five years and the tribal members were to become citizens of Kansas. In 1867, however, the Ottawa signed the Omnibus Treaty allowing them to purchase land from the Shawnee along the Neosho River in Ottawa County. Their tribal headquarters is at Miami.

Some Ojibway also joined the Ottawa. The Ojibway were once one of the largest tribes in North America and were spread along the American-Canadian border between North Dakota and the Great Lakes. In the early eighteenth century several bands of Ojibways consolidated with the Ottawa and later removed to Kansas. In 1859, two other bands of Ojibway confederated with the Munsee, who moved into the Cherokee Nation from Kansas in 1867. Other bands of Ojibway joined the Potawatomi and were resettled in Pottawatomie County.

Another band settling in northeastern Oklahoma was the Confederated Peoria, one of the principal tribes of the Illinois Confederacy. The Peoria were joined by the Cahokia, Moingwena, Michigamea,

Tamaroa, and Kaskaskia after a long period of warfare had decimated these tribes. In 1832, the Peoria and their allies gave up their land in Illinois and Missouri and were assigned a reservation on the Osage River in Kansas. In 1849, the Peoria, Kaskaskia, Wea, Piankshaw, Cahokia, Moingwena, Michigamea, and Tamaroa formed a new confederacy, and when federal officials recognized the union in 1854 the tribe was known as the Confederated Peoria.

In 1867 the Confederated Peoria signed the Omnibus Treaty providing for the sale of their land in Kansas and their removal to Indian Territory. The Confederated Peoria's new reservaton was purchased from the Quapaw and Shawnee in present-day Ottawa County. In 1873, the Confederate Peoria were united with the Miami and renamed the United Peoria and Miami. Tribal headquarters is at Miami in Ottawa County.

The Miami were from Wisconsin, but the tribe migrated south and settled along the Miami and Walbash rivers in Ohio and Illinois. At the close of the French and Indian War in 1763, they abandoned their holdings in Ohio and moved to Indiana. Intermittent warfare with encroaching whites continued through the War of 1812. No longer able to stem the white encroachment, the Miami sold their lands in Indiana in 1840 and accepted a 500,000-acre reservation in Kansas; by 1847 most tribal members were settled along the banks of the Marais des Cygnes River in Kansas. With the settlement of Kansas, pressure was put on the Miami to move again, and in 1867 the tribe was offered two alternatives: either become citizens of Kansas or move to Indian Territory and become confederated with the Peoria, Kaskaskia, Wea, and Piankashaw. Seventy-two Miami agreed to move and were settled with the Peoria in Ottawa County where they were known as the United Peoria and Miami. In 1940 a federal charter was granted to the tribe, which maintains its headquarters at Miami.

The Eel River Indians were joined with the Miami in 1839. Originally they lived along the Eel River in western Indiana. They took part in the uprising in the Ohio River Valley during the War of 1812 and afterward they were herded onto a reservation in Boone County, Indiana, which they sold when they merged with the Miami. In 1846-1847 they were removed to Kansas with the Miami, and in 1867 they were resettled with the Miami in Ottawa County.

Originally a part of the Osage tribe, the Quapaw separated and established their own villages near the mouth of the Arkansas River and north along the west bank of the Mississippi River. Later the tribe moved up the Arkansas River and claimed much of southern Arkansas and Oklahoma and northern Louisiana. In 1833, the Quapaw accepted a 150-square mile reservation near the Seneca in Ottawa County. About one-third of the tribe move to Ottawa County, while the remainder moved into the Choctaw and Creek nations. After the Civil War the Quapaw moved into the Osage Reservation, and in 1867 they ceded their lands in Kansas and some of the lands in Indian Territory to the federal government. In 1878, all but 35 Quapaw were living with the Osage. Tribal headquarters is at Quapaw in Ottawa County.

One of the last of the tribes forcibly removed to Oklahoma were the Modoc of southwestern Oregon and northwestern California. In 1864 they were forced onto a reservation along the Klamath River in Oregon.

ported to the Quapaw Agency in Indian Territory. In June of 1874, the federal government purchased 4,040 acres for the Modoc from the Eastern Shawnee in Ottawa County. In 1909, Congress enacted legislation allowing the Modoc to return to the Klamath Reservation. Those opting to return were placed on the Modoc of Oregon tribal rolls. The band split, with some returning to the West Coast and others remaining in Oklahoma. Those remaining in Oklahoma maintain their tribal headquarters at Miami in Ottawa County.

With the decision to assimilate Native Americans into the mainstream of American culture the federal government began a policy to eliminate tribal authority completely. The Plains Indians of western Oklahoma were the first to feel the effects of this new policy. Their reservations were divided among tribal members in allotments, and the remaining lands were opened to homesteaders through a series of land runs and lotteries. Once the Indian title to the area was eliminated, this region formed what was organized into Oklahoma Territory.

JIM ARGO

The Indian blanket, Oklahoma's official state wildflower.

Led by Captain Jack, a group of Modoc left the Klamath Reservation in 1870 and returned to their old homeland in California. The result was the Modoc War of 1872-1873. Jack was hanged for his part in the uprising and his followers were moved to Fort McPherson, Nebraska. From there they were trans-

In an attempt to maintain control over their own affairs, the tribes in eastern Oklahoma attempted to form the State of Sequoyah from the Indian nations, but failed to receive any support on the national level. Afterward, their lands were allotted and the region added to Oklahoma Territory to form the state of Oklahoma.

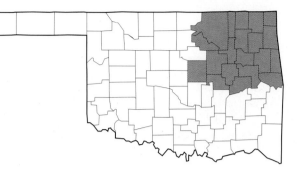

BLACK GOLD IN THE RED MAN'S LAND

NORTHEASTERN OKLAHOMA

Northeastern Oklahoma is one of the richest energy producing regions in North America, and is the location of several of the largest oil discoveries ever made in the United States. It is in the center of the Mid-Continent Oil and Gas region stretching from Kansas to East Texas. Between 1900 and 1935, Mid-Continent ranked first among the nation's oil-producers twenty-seven times. Hundreds of millions of dollars in oil gushed from beneath northeastern Oklahoma. The tremendous wealth touched off the last great mineral rush to the American West as tens of thousands of wildcatters, roughnecks, prostitutes, gamblers, and bootleggers joined the rush for riches. Boom towns appeared and disappeared overnight as the Oklahoma oil boom produced more money than the California and Colorado gold rushes combined.

The region's oil deposits were well-known to Native Americans. New Spring Place, an oil spring near Oaks in Delaware County, was used by Indians for medicinal purposes. The state's first oil well was drilled in 1859, when Lewis Ross struck oil while sinking a saltwater well at the Grand Saline in Mayes County. In 1887 Edward Byrd formed the United States Oil and Gas Company that drilled eleven wells along Oil Branch Creek in Rogers County. The first well was completed in 1889 and flowed half a barrel of oil daily. Oklahoma's first commercially successful oil well, The Nellie Johnston No. 1, was completed by Michael Cudahy near Bartlesville in 1897.

These early successes led to the opening of the Cherokee Shallow Sand District in Nowata and Rogers counties, in 1904. The Red Fork Oil Field, south of the Arkansas River from Tulsa, was the first major commercial field developed in Indian Territory. Its discovery well, the Sue A. Bland No. 1, was named for the Creek wife of Dr. John C. Bland, who along with John Wick, Jesse A. Heydrick, and Dr. Fred S. Clinton financed the venture. Within a month one thousand oilmen flocked to the town of Red Fork, which at the time rivaled Tulsa. The discovery prompted the con-

JIM ARGO

One of the thousands of pumping units of the oil-rich Osage.

struction of the Eleventh Street Bridge between Tulsa and Red Fork by a group of Tulsa investors. It launched Tulsa on the road to becoming the "Oil Capital of the World."

Located in eastern Pawnee County, the Cleveland Oil Field was the first major strike in Oklahoma Territory. Creekology—the primary method of locating oil before the refinement of the science of geology—held that because oil and water do not mix, streams flow around underground deposits of crude. Therefore, the best place to drill was in the bend of a river. The Cleveland strike was made in 1904 by the Mennetonka Oil and Gas Company in the center of the large bend of the Arkansas River north of the town of Cleveland.

Located in Oklahoma Territory, where alcohol was allowed, Cleveland became a major source for supplies and liquor for oilmen across the Arkansas River in Indian Territory, where alcohol was banned. The community once boasted eleven saloons and three distilleries. One of the major developers of the pool was the Minnehoma Oil Company owned by George F. Getty and his son, J. Paul Getty, who later formed Getty Oil and became known as the "richest man in the world."

The Hogshooter Natural Gas Field, opened in 1907 in Washington County, was the first significant "dry" gas discovery in Oklahoma. "Dry" gas is not produced in association with crude, while "wet" gas generally is found with oil. Between Bristow and Stroud is one of the nation's most extensive underground natural gas storage facilities. Developed by the Oklahoma Natural Gas Company, it is capable of storing 75 billion cubic feet of natural gas.

The discovery that launched the Oklahoma oil boom was made in 1905 on the Ida Glenn farm south of Tulsa, that Robert Galbreath leased for three cents per acre. The Glenn Pool Oil Field was the twentieth-largest oil find in the United States prior to 1950, with an output of almost 239 million barrels of crude. Its discovery well, the Ida Glenn No. 1, was completed by Galbreath and Frank Chelsey in October 1905. The strike resulted in such companies as The Texas Company (Texaco) and Gulf tying the state into their pipeline network and providing Oklahoma oilmen with their first major marketing outlet. The strike also touched off a major oil rush to the area by thousands of Eastern oilmen.

Kiefer, in Creek County, was one of the state's wildest oil boom towns. At the height of the Glenn Pool boom, Kiefer had a population of 10,000, many of them being prostitutes, gamblers and bootleggers who inhabited that section of the town known as the Bowery, home to numerous saloons, brothels, dance halls and gambling dens. In 1909, the D.W. Franchot Company operated the first successful gas processing plant in Oklahoma east of Kiefer.

One of the major communities in the Glenn Pool

Field was Sapulpa, which means "sweet potato" in the Creek language. Both the Frankhoma Pottery Plant and the Liberty Glass Company call Sapulpa home. Their founders were attracted to the area by the plentiful supply of natural gas that was used to fuel their plants. One of the major developers of the Glenn Pool Field was Charles Page, who founded the Sand Spring Home for Homeless Children in 1908 and then the town of Sand Springs to support the home.

With these nearby discoveries, Tulsa, the county seat of Tulsa County, mushroomed overnight from a small Creek village called Tulsey Town—from the Creek word *tallasi* (town)—into a major energy center. Placed north of the strike at Glenn Pool, Tulsa became a mecca for oilmen such as Henry F. Sinclair, J. Paul Getty, William K. Skelly and Waite Phillips and the home to such energy firms as Skelly Oil, Cities Service and The Williams Brothers.

Tulsa was the home of W.F. (Billy) Rosser, the owner of the Oklahoma State Oil Company, the Ethel Oil Company and the Coast Oil Company. His income was $3,000 per day before his luck ran out and he found himself broke. Starting over, he built a second fortune only to go broke once again. In all he made and lost $50 million. Another Tulsa oil pioneer was William K. Warren, who founded Warren Petroleum in 1922. In 1955, the company was purchased by the Gulf Oil Corporation in what was then the largest exchange of money in the history of the oil industry. Joshua. S. Cosden, known as the "Prince of Petroleum," made and lost two oil fortunes. Cosden used his fortune to make Tulsa a major refining center and built the town's first skyscraper—the Mid-Continent Building. Another Tulsa landmark is the Boston Avenue Methodist Church, the world's first church built to cathedral scale in skyscraper style.

At one time Tulsa claimed six refineries, including the huge Texas Company complex in West Tulsa. For years it hosted the International Petroleum Exposition and Congress—the largest meeting of oilmen in the world. It also is the home of the University of Tulsa, whose School of Petroleum Geology, opened in 1928, is internationally known. Tulsa also is the home of the *Oil & Gas Journal*, often called the "Oilman's Bible."

The American Association of Petroleum Geologists, organized in 1915, is a Tulsa-based organization recognized worldwide. The Oklahoma Petroleum Council was organized in Tulsa in 1919. In 1982, it merged with the Kansas-Oklahoma Division of the Mid-Continent Oil and Gas Association. The Association of Natural Gasoline Manufacturers, now called the Gas Processors Association, was organized in Tulsa in 1921.

Modern Tulsa still is a major energy center with the $200 million Williams Center dominating its skyline and more than 850 energy-related businesses op erating in the community. Moreover, it is a leading cultural influence on the state. Tulsa contains two of the nation's finest museums—the Thomas Gilcrease Institute of American History and Art, and Philbrook Art Center—and four major institutions of higher education—the University of Tulsa, Oral Roberts University, Tulsa Junior College and the University Center at Tulsa.

North of Tulsa was the Osage Reservation, which contained one of the largest concentrations of oil fields ever discovered in America. The entire 2,286-square-mile reservation was leased by Henry

hijackers who stopped automobiles struggling up the steep incline.

One of the largest discoveries in the Osage was the Burbank Oil Field, which produced more than 228 million barrels of oil between 1920 and 1950. It was the 21st-largest field uncovered during that time span. The production was so great that the Midland Oil Company had paid $1.99 million for a single 160-acre lease. Another Osage oil boom town, Hominy, contains the Drummond Home, built in 1905. The Fairfax Cemetery, set on a hill to the west of that town's main street, contains numerous ornate head-

Foster on March 14, 1896. To develop the property, Henry's brother Edwin organized the Phenix Oil Company and then the Indian Territory Illuminating Oil Company (ITIO), forerunner of Cities Service Oil Company. In 1901, Henry V. Foster, the son of Henry Foster, assumed control of the operation, which was based in Bartlesville.

The Osage spawned a number of oil boom towns. Pershing was the site of Phillips Petroleum Company's 10,000-barrel-per-day refinery complex. The ruins of the Pershing First Baptist Church and an abandoned school building are all that remain of the community. DeNoya located just south of Shidler used to be called Whizbang, perhaps because, as one early-day oilman said, it whizzed all day and banged all night. The remains of the Adams Hotel, the Liberty Theater and the concrete foundations of the local school still can be seen. Northeast of Whizbang, Pistol Hill was a favorite place for

The Muscogee & Fort Gibson stagecoach fording the Arkansas River two miles below Fort Gibson in 1890.

Left: A roughneck using a spinning chain to join two stems of drill pipe together.

Below: The Golden Driller in front of the Exposition Center, long a familiar sight at the International Petroleum Exposition in Tulsa. Such gatherings of oilmen from throughout the world helped make Tulsa the "Oil Capital of the World."

Above: *The Williams Center and Samson Plaza in Tulsa. The revitalization of downtown Tulsa has turned the area into a showcase of modern urban planning.*

Above: *Price Tower in Bartlesville. Designed by Frank Lloyd Wright, the structure incorporated many unique features of engineering and design.*

Left: *The Boston Avenue Methodist Church in Tulsa. The massive limestone wall of the main building stands four stories high.*

FRED W. MARVEL/OK TOURISM

NORTHEASTERN OKLAHOMA —————— 35

stones, including a life-size statue of Chief Ne-Kah-Wah-She-Tun-Kah, who served four terms as governor of the Osage Nation.

The seat of Osage County and the capital of the Osage Nation, Pawhuska, was the center of the boom. The Church of the Immaculate Conception has a special dispensation from the Catholic Church to portray the history of the Osage Nation in its stained glass windows. The Triangle Building was the base of operations for many Osage oilmen. Under the "Million Dollar Elm" on the grounds of the Osage Agency, Colonel E.E. Walters held many of the Osage lease sales. These auctions of the Osage's prime oil lands poured millions of dollars into the tribe's treasury. Walters lived in Skedee, just across the Arkansas River from the Osage in Pawnee County. Little remains of the community except the life-size statue of Osage Chief Bacon Rind, erected in 1926 by Walters as a gesture of his friendship to the Osage.

At the time of allotment, the Osage Nation insisted that the tribal mineral rights be reserved for the benefit of the tribe as a whole. As a result, each of the 2,229 Osage headrights held an equal share of the tribe's oil's wealth. Between 1901 and 1950, a sum of almost $300 million was divided among the Osage, making them the "richest Indians in the world." This concentration of money led to the Osage Reign of Terror—masterminded by William K. Hale—during which Osages were murdered to gain control of their headrights.

The Osage also gave birth to the Phillips Petroleum Company, organized by Frank and L.E. Phillips in 1917. Fourteen years earlier the two brothers had arrived in Bartlesville and quickly became involved in the Osage oil boom. On September 6, 1905, the Anna Anderson No. 1 was completed and was Phillips Petroleum's first gusher in the region. Today Phillips Petroleum Company is still headquartered in Bartlesville.

The Bartlesville Energy Technology Center was opened in 1919 by Phillips Petroleum and has played a major role in the advancement of petroleum technology. In addition, George P. Bunn and F.E. Rice of Phillips Petroleum Company pioneered the development of the nation's natural gas industry. Their work, *Natural Gasoline*, became the mainstay of the industry and allowed Phillips Petroleum to become an international leader in the natural gas industry, controlling one-fourth of the nation's natural gasoline production. Bartlesville's best known landmark is the Price Tower, designed by Frank Lloyd Wright. Southwest of Bartlesville is Woolaroc, a 4,000-acre ranch featuring exotic animals, an outstanding museum, and Phillips Lodge, built in 1927 as Frank Phillips' country home.

H.L. Doherty of the Empire Oil & Gas Company (a forerunner of Cities Service) and John C. Walker pioneered the process of refining natural gas liquid and turned the company's research plant at Tallant, in Osage County, into the major petrochemical research facility in America.

The Cushing-Drumright Oil Field in Creek County was the tenth-largest oil discovery made in America prior to 1950 and between 1912 and 1919 produced 3 percent of the world's crude. It was discovered by Tom Slick in 1912 on the Frank Wheeler farm. Slick rushed to Cushing, the closest town, and leased all available automobiles, wagons and teams so that other oilmen could not reach the well site before he leased the adjoining land.

Many Indians and freedmen of the area suddenly found themselves wealthy. Jackson Barnett's allotment produced $24 million worth of crude, while Sarah Rector, the descendant of a slave, received $300,000 for her quarter section.

Because of the huge amount of money generated by the rush to develop the pool, the region became the location of some of the state's wildest oil boom towns. Drumright in Creek County was notorious: men fought to the finish in the mud and dust of Tiger Creek Avenue. Eventually the violence became so bad that area oilmen raised $5,000 to hire law officers to tame the town.

Boasting its Irish heritage, nearby Shamrock named its streets Cork, Dublin, Kilarney and Tipperary, and a green stripe was used to divide traffic. Its local newspaper was called the *Shamrock Brogue,* and local residents imported a blarney stone from Ireland. Other nearby boom towns were Dropright, Allright, Damnright, Justright and Gasright.

Disaster struck the region in 1914. Because of the huge production in the field, hundreds of thousands of barrels of crude were stored in open-pit tanks and dammed creek beds. On August 8, 1914, the field was swept by a series of electrical storms and lightning set several of the pits on fire. The flames burned for days, blacking out the sun with oily smoke before firefighters brought the fires under control. The waste was so great that the Oklahoma Corporation Commission issued its famous Order No. 829, one of the first energy conservation regulations in the nation.

It was northeastern Oklahoma's mineral wealth that first attracted non-Indians to the region. As early as 1718 Frenchmen from New Orleans made their way up the Mississippi-Arkansas river system to the Three Forks area—where the Arkansas, Grand and Verdigris rivers join—in search of lead. They may not, however, have been the first non-Indians to penetrate the area. At Heavener, the state maintains the Heavener Runestone State Park, where in 1912 on the side of nearby Mount Poteau a thick slab of sandstone was found covered with runic letters. Some historians believe that the rune stone marks a visit to the region by a Viking exploring party in 1017.

Fur quickly replaced lead as the primary resource of the area and several trading posts were established. Fort Fabry, near Calvin in Hughes County, was built by Fabry de Bruyere in 1741. Fabry and the other traders used pirogues—crude vessels made by hollowing cottonwood tree trunks—to transport their goods. Later, flatboats were introduced. Nothing but barges, they were constructed near the riverbank and then launched to drift downstream to markets. Auguste P. Chouteau maintained a boatyard at his trading post at the falls of the Verdigris, near its confluence with the Arkansas River and near Sam Houston's 1830's trading post. In 1824, Chouteau constructed sufficient flatboats to ship 1,938 packs and bales of fur to New Orleans.

Several other trading settlements were established in the area, including one in 1819 by Nathaniel Pryor in Mayes County that still bears his name. Nearby is Salina, where Jean Pierre Chouteau established his trading post in 1796. The nearby town of Choteau is named for the Chouteau family, who became a major influence in the area. When Auguste P. Chouteau, son of Jean Pierre Chouteau, died in 1838, Cherokee Chief John Ross acquired his home and in 1872 it was converted into the Cherokee Orphan Asylum. Sallisaw, in Sequoyah County, began as a trading post along the Fort Gibson to Fort Smith road.

Missionaries closely followed the fur traders. In 1830 the Presbyterians established Dwight Mission, near Sallisaw, to serve local Cherokees. Another early-day mission was Tullasassee in Wagoner County. Established in 1850 by E.M. Loughridge, it was the major educational facility in the Creek Nation. It burned in 1880 but was rebuilt as a school for Creek freedmen.

Following the Civil War, Reconstruction Treaties granted the newly freed slaves portions of the tribal domain. These freedmen became an important part of the region's culture and founded several all-black communities. Among them were Boley, which once claimed to be the largest all-black town in America; Clearview, also known as Abelincoln; and Taft. When Lelia Foley was elected mayor of Taft in 1874, she became the first black woman elected to the office of mayor in America.

To allow movement both upstream or downstream, keelboats were introduced in 1821 by Thomas James. Large craft, they could carry as much as 20 tons or 100 passengers. In deep water they were pulled upstream by a method known as cordelling. In shallower water, the keelboats were poled up river at an average daily rate of progression of about 15 miles.

In 1820, river traffic in Oklahoma was revolutionized when the *Comet* became the first steamboat to arrive at Fort Smith. Two years later, the *Robert Thompson* opened regular steamboat service to Fort Smith.

For six years, Fort Smith remained the head of steamboat navigation on the Arkansas. In 1828, however, the steamboat *Facility* succeeded in pushing 65 miles farther upstream to Frozen Rock, the landing at Fort Gibson.

Fort Gibson was established in 1824 on the east side of Grand River. At that time it was the westernmost American military post. Several buildings were constructed, including barracks, officers' quarters, a commissary, guard house, hospital, chapel and two blockhouses. During the Mexican War it served as a staging area for American troops marching south, and was the final destination for the Cherokees on the Trail of Tears. The post was abandoned in 1857, but when federal troops reoccupied the northern Indian Territory in 1863, Union Colonel William A. Phillips regarrisoned the post, expanded its defenses and named the complex Fort Blunt. In 1871 Fort Gibson was transformed into a transportation depot. It was closed permanently in 1890.

To counteract the federal presence at Fort Blunt, in November 1862 the Confederates constructed Fort Davis on top of a 25-foot-tall prehistoric Indian mound on the south side of the Arkansas River north of Bacone College. It was occupied intermittently until 1862, when federal forces burned it. Other early-day military posts in northeastern Oklahoma included Fort Arbuckle on the Arkansas and Fort Wayne.

Northeastern Oklahoma was a battleground between Union and Confederate troops throughout the Civil War. Early in the fighting the South drove the pro-Northern Creek Indians, led by Opothleyahola, into exile in a series of three battles in November and December 1862: Chusto-Talasah, or Caving Banks, fought in a horseshoe bend in Bird Creek in Tulsa County, Round Mountain along the Payne-Pawnee county line, and Chustenahlah in Osage County west of Skiatook.

There were several other important Civil War battles in northeastern Oklahoma. In July 1863 Confederate Brigadier General Stand Watie, the only Native American to attain the rank of general in the Civil War, unsuccessfully attempted to seize a federal wagon train where the California Road crossed Cabin Creek in Mayes County in the First Battle of Cabin Creek. The Second Battle of Cabin Creek took place at the same location in September 1864. This time Watie succeeded, capturing a federal wagon train valued at $1.5 million. The Battle of Honey Springs, the largest Civil War battle fought in Oklahoma, took place in July 1863 along Elk Creek in McIntosh and Muskogee counties, and broke the power of the Confederacy in Indian Territory. The final major Confederate victory in the area was the capture of the *J.R. Williams* by Stand Watie near Pleasant Bluff in Haskell County in June 1864.

Right: Water flowing over the rim of the deep canyon on Poteau Mountain near Heavener where the Heavener Runestone was discovered in 1912. The 12-foot-high, 10-foot-wide, 2-foot-thick slab of sandstone is covered with eight deeply carved runic letters.
Below: French mulberry growing wild in the Heavener Runestone State Park in LeFlore County.

Facing page, top: The two-story white frame birthplace of Will Rogers, famed humorist, in the Will Rogers State Park at Oologah.

Above: *The home of Waite Phillips, a pioneer Oklahoma oilman, and the surrounding 23 acres and accompanying formal gardens, was converted into the Philbrook Art Center in 1938.*

Right: *Goat's Bluff on the Illinois River. One of America's last free-flowing and scenic streams is a mecca for canoeist and fisherman.*

Steamboats such as the *J.R. Williams* were constantly in danger from snags and submerged obstacles and used the Arkansas River only during the boating season in the spring and the fall of the year. The main barrier to navigation on the upper Arkansas was Webbers Falls, which in the nineteenth century actually was a falls on the Arkansas River at the mouth of Illinois River. Even in the wet season it sometimes was necessary to tow smaller craft over the falls using yokes of oxen. Other more powerful vessels often jumped the falls by ramming them with sufficient speed to be hurled over the obstruction. Webbers Falls is nothing but a ripple in the Arkansas River today.

The Splitlog Church at Cayuga, built by Mathias Splitlog, a Wyandotte Indian.

River transportation in Oklahoma was revitalized in 1970 with the opening of the McClellan-Kerr Arkansas River Navigation System, a $1.3 billion, 445-mile-long waterway that provided a reliable, year-around route into Oklahoma from the Mississippi River. Two river ports operate on the Oklahoma portion of the project—Muskogee and Catoosa.

Muskogee lies in the heart of the Three Forks country, and was established with the removal of the Creek Nation to the region in the 1820s. Their agency was located to the northwest at Fern Mountain. Muskogee, a major stopover on the Texas Road, was the site of the first federal jail built in Indian Territory. Its future was assured with the arrival of the Missouri-Kansas-Texas Railroad in 1872, and quickly developed into a major cultural and commercial center. In 1874 the Union Agency was established in Muskogee to oversee the affairs of the Five Tribes. Today the agency building is maintained as the Five Civilized Tribes Museum. Bacone Indian College was moved to Muskogee in 1885. The institution's Native American Art School and the Ataloa Lodge Indian Museum are internationally recognized.

Northeastern Oklahoma also is the location of the Tri-State Lead and Zinc Mining District. By the mid-1920s the Oklahoma portion of the district was producing almost $50 million of lead and zinc annually. Lead and zinc mining in the Commerce area began in 1907, and within two years the field had produced almost $4.8 million worth of ore. The Turkey Fat Mine actually conducted mining operations within the town limits.

Another mining town is Miami, which, as the site of the Quapaw Indian Agency, oversaw the leasing of Indian mineral rights. In 1926, the Kansas Explorations Company paid John Quapaw $105,000 for six acres. This was the largest lease payment made in the region. In 1919 the Oklahoma School of Mines (Northeastern Oklahoma A & M College) was opened in Miami.

By 1915, the Pitcher Lead and Zinc Field was responsible for 90 percent of the district's production, and Pitcher was the site of the largest lead and zinc mining complex in the world. One of the state's wildest boom towns, it was also the home of the Eagle Pitcher Lead and Zinc Company, which dominated the region's activity.

In addition to lead and zinc, northeastern Oklahoma is a major supplier of coal. Opened to coal production in 1903 to provide fuel for railroads, the Henryetta Coal Mining District claimed such coal towns as Bryan, Coalton, Dewar, Grayson, Kusa and Schulter. Henryetta became a major mineral center of the region with the completion of a zinc smelter and a cadmium and germanium refinery. The community traditionally has been the "Labor Capital of Oklahoma," and its annual Labor Day celebration has attracted thousands of participants. Reflecting the early-day labor movement of the region were the songs of Woody Guthrie. Born in 1912 in Okemah, just to the west of Henryetta, the famed folk singer is internationally recognized as the balladeer of the Depression years.

Combined with northeastern Oklahoma's mineral wealth is its natural beauty. The wooded hillsides of the Cookson Hills, Boston Mountains, Ozark Mountains and Osage Hills are covered with oak, pine, redbud and dogwood, and a myriad of wildflowers. The hills are a burst of color during the fall months. Spread among these hills are a number of state parks and lakes including: Grand Lake O' the Cherokees, Lake Spavinaw, Lake Eucha, Fort Gibson Lake, Lake Tenkiller, Greenleaf Lake, Lake Keystone, Kaw Lake, Markham Ferry Lake and Lake Eufaula. The Illinois River which flows through the region attracts thousands of tourists annually. Together with Flint Creek and Barren Fork Creek, the Illinois has been designated a scenic river.

Among the best-known locations on the Illinois River is Tahlequah, capital of th e Cherokee Nation. The tribe's capitol building, supreme court building and national jail still stand. It was at Tahlequah that Cherokee Brigadier General Stand Watie raised the Southern banner at the outbreak of the Civil War and organized the Cherokee Mounted Rifles for service in the Confederate Army. Tahlequah is also the home of Northeastern Oklahoma State University. South of Tahlequah is Park Hill, one of the state's oldest and historically significant communities. It was the site of the Cherokee Female Seminary that burned in 1887; however, the seminary's brick columns remain as a part of the Cherokee National Museum and Tsa-La-Gi complex.

It was along the main rivers and their tributaries in northeastern Oklahoma that many of the state's earliest settlements were established. Bitting Springs Mill used its French burrs turned by a wooden water wheel to grind cornmeal. Hildebrand Mill along Flint Creek in Delaware County was another early-day community. Nearby is Dripping Springs, one of Oklahoma's few natural waterfalls. Cayuga, northeast of Grove in Delaware County, was the home of Mathias Splitlog. A wealthy man, Splitlog constructed several industries along Cowskin Creek, including a flour mill, sawmill and a wagon works. To connect his businesses with markets in Missouri, Splitlog built the "Splitlog Railroad." He also helped finance the Splitlog Church, which still stands and is on the National Register of Historic Places.

Northeastern Oklahoma is the home of one of America's greatest humorists, Will Rogers, who was born northeast of Oologah in Rogers County. Will Rogers State Park, featuring the birthplace of Rogers, is located northeast of the town along the shores of Oologah Reservoir. Adjacent to the reservoir is the 16,310-acre Oologah Public Hunting Area. The Will Rogers Memorial is located in Claremore. The memorial's best known feature is its duplicate of Jo Davidson's famed statue of Rogers, as well as mementos of Rogers' life. Claremore is also the home of the impressive J.M. Davis Gun Museum and the Oklahoma Military Academy, now Rogers State College. The school houses the Lynn Riggs Memorial, honoring the author of *Green Grow the Lilacs* adapted for the long-running musical *Oklahoma!*

Pawnee was the home of another world traveler and entertainer, Gordon W. "Pawnee Bill" Lillie. Lillie first came to Indian Territory in 1882, where he worked as a stockman, Indian trader and scout. Well-known among the Pawnee, Lillie organized the Pawnee Bill Wild West Show, which regularly toured America and Europe. Headquarters for the show was Blue Hawk Peak near Pawnee where Lillie built his home, now open for touring. Moreover, Pawnee was the boyhood home of Chester Gould, creator of the Dick Tracy; the site of Pawnee Bill Trading Post, exporter of authentic Native American artifacts; and the Pawnee Indian Powwow, one of the largest gatherings of Indian dancers in the nation.

Northeastern Oklahoma's mineral wealth gave birth to the last great mineral rush to the American West, creating a myriad of boom towns that rivaled the California gold rush and financing the emergence of the area into a major cultural center—a culture that blends Native American traditions with such ethnic diversity as Prague's annual Czechoslovakian Koloche Festival, and a scenic beauty of lakes and wooded hills.

Above: *Price Falls in the Arbuckle Mountains is one of many natural waterfalls in the region.*

Facing page: *Honey Creek flowing through the Arbuckle Mountains in Murray County. The Arbuckles are one of the oldest mountain chains in the world and are little more than eroded stumps of once lofty peaks.*

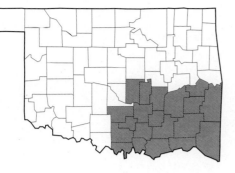

LITTLE DIXIE
SOUTHEASTERN OKLAHOMA

The beautiful Ouachita and Arbuckle mountains are the dominant geographical features of southeastern Oklahoma. A westward counterpart of the Appalachian Valley and Ridge Area, the Ouachitas have the greatest relief of any mountains in Oklahoma. The topography of the region makes it one of the most isolated regions of the state, which created a pattern of settlement much like Appalachia—isolated settlements set in deep valleys.

The natural beauty of the dense forest is preserved in the Ouachita National Forest. More than 75 streams pass through the forest, as does the famous Talihina Trail, Oklahoma State Highway 1, which attracts thousands of motorists along the Kiamichi River to look at the autumnal leaves. There are several state parks and national recreation areas in the region. Robbers' Cave State Park in the heart of the San Bois Mountains is one of the most popular. The cave itself, located 100 feet up the side of a sandstone cliff, was a hideout for outlaws who flocked to the region that used to be outside of any state or territorial jurisdiction.

Beavers Bend State Park is on the shore of Broken Bow Lake, a 14,200-acre reservoir formed by the state's highest dam. Nearby are the 14,078-acre McCurtain County Wilderness Area and a 5,420-acre state game preserve. The Glover River, which flows through the area, provides some of the best free-flowing water in the nation for canoeing.

Little remains of the once massive Arbuckle Mountains. Their sharply ribbed edges of limestone are contorted by a complex system of faults and folds that attract geologists worldwide. Two of the most popular attractions of the Arbuckles are Turner and Price falls, south of Davis. Other nearby falls include the Seven Sisters, Burning Mountain, and Price Falls, the home of Falls Creek, a well-known Baptist youth camp.

Along the Red River, between the Ouachita and Arbuckle mountains, is Lake Texhoma, a 88,000-acre reservoir created by the damming of the Red River. Its 580 miles of shoreline are ringed with recreational facilities, including the 1,884-acre Lake Texhoma State Park.

The mountains of southeastern Oklahoma are rich in coal. Bernard de la Harpe first reported coal in Pittsburg County in 1719. It was not until 1872,

STEVE MULLIGAN

however, that commercial coal mining started, when the Osage Coal and Mining Company opened a mine at Krebs to supply fuel for the Missouri, Kansas and Texas Railroad. Other coal companies quickly followed. McAlester—named for J.J. McAlester, "father of the Oklahoma coal mining industry"—quickly overshadowed Krebs as the center of the region's coal industry. In 1889, coal mines were opened at Hartshorne, whose population reached 2,352 within a year.

McAlester also is the location of the McAlester

Left: *Picking cotton in "Little Dixie." Corn and cotton dominated the agricultural economy of southeastern Oklahoma during the 18th century. In the center of the photograph is the scale used for weighing the bags of cotton. Workers were paid on the weight of cotton picked each day.*

Center: *Early-day settlers enjoying a swim in Pennington Creek near Tishomingo. A portion of the spring-fed stream flows through a series of rapids, cataracts, and falls known as "Devil's Den."*

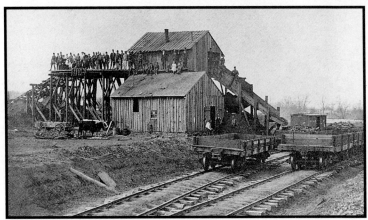

Left: *One of the many coal mines that once occupied the McAlester area. In this photograph the workers of Mine No. 9 are watching coal being loaded onto a Missouri, Kansas, and Texas coal car. Many of the early miners were European immigrants, which gives the region a distintive ethnic culture.*

Consistory of Scottish Rite Masonry and Rainbow Temple, which serves as the headquarters of the International Order of Rainbow Girls. The temple is topped by a copper sphere containing 168 multicolored illuminated windows. This "Light of Masonry," is visible for a great distance. In addition, McAlester was the location of the Tobucksy County Courthouse, which dispensed Choctaw justice from 1876 until 1907, and is site of the Oklahoma State Penitentiary.

Mining in the Coalgate Coal District began in 1882 along the main street of the town of Coalgate. Another nearby coal town, Lehigh, was named the seat of Coal County at statehood in 1907, but in 1908, voters moved the seat to Coalgate. The Eastern Coal Mining District included the anthracite coal deposits in northern LeFlore County and bituminous mines in the southern part of the county. Howe once was the largest settlement on the Chicago, Rock Island and Pacific Railroad between McAlester and Memphis, Tennessee. Opened in 1903, the Henryetta Coal District was developed to provide fuel for the St. Louis and San Francisco and Kansas, Oklahoma and Gulf railroads.

Many of the early coal miners were immigrants from England, Scotland, Wales, Ireland, Italy, Germany, Lithuania, Poland, Austria-Hungary and Russia. The various ethnic groups settled together. Krebs was a center of settlement for Italian miners. In addition, a large number of blacks entered the coal mines in the post-Civil War era.

Miners sometimes worked on their knees in the low shafts; in the absence of an adequate ventilation system, the shafts filled with foul air and coal dust. Such conditions contributed to frequent accidents. In January 1879, in the state's worst coal mine disaster, an explosion in Osage Coal and Mining Company's Mine No. 11 at Krebs killed 87 miners. In 1992, the First National Bank of McAlester commissioned a statue and memorial wall honoring the pioneer coal miners of the area.

A series of long and bitter labor disputes ended the coal mining era. When strikers walked off the job in May 1894, the mines stopped paying the monthly tax required by the Choctaws for non-Indian miners. The tribe declared the miners intruders and federal troops deported 200 of the strikers. Another series of strikes between 1898 and 1904 resulted in many of the miners being replaced by black miners from Alabama. Another strike, from 1923 to 1929, closed most of the mines.

Coal was not the only mineral mined in southeastern Oklahoma. Jumbo, northwest of Antlers in Pushmataha County, was an asphalt-mining boom town in the 1890s. A mine fire in 1905 and an explosion in 1910 destroyed both the industry and the town's future.

The heavily wooded terrain of southeastern Oklahoma also encouraged an extensive lumber industry. The logging industry started shortly after the arrival of the Choctaws and Chickasaws in the region and increased following the Civil War. In 1868, Choctaw Chief Allen Wright opened the first steam-powered sawmill in the area at Boggy Depot. When the Missouri, Kansas and Texas Railroad was completed in 1872, a ready means to market timber was available and several lumber towns were developed.

Stringtown once contained twenty-two sawmills. At Rodney, on the Kiamichi River, the sawmill was powered by an overshoot waterwheel fed by a dam. The Long-Bell Lumber Company mill at Antlers could produce 150,000 board feet of lumber daily and was fed by a ten-mile-long tramway into the wooded mountains. The Stamp Mill, the Fort Towson Lumber Company and Pine Belt Lumber Company were other major employers. America, Big Cedar, Bokhoma, Millerton, Tom, Glover and Eagletown became major timber towns.

In 1888, the Choctaw Lumber and Coal Company began its timber operations, and by 1910 it was operating sawmills in Wright City and Broken Bow. The Wright City operation produced 125,000 board feet of pine daily and the Broken Bow mill an additional 60,000 feet of hardwood. To ship its products to market, the company built a private railroad through the area. In 1921 the Dierks Lumber Company acquired the Choctaw Lumber and Coal Company. The Dierks brothers had been involved in southeastern Oklahoma's lumbering operations for several years. In 1911 they had founded the town of Beavers Bend and erected a nearby lumber mill in 1912. A center of the state's lumber industry, Beavers Bend is the location of the Forest Heritage Center.

In 1969, the Dierks operations were merged with Weyerhaeuser Corporation. Weyerhaeuser eventually acquired title to about half of the land in McCurtain County. Weyerhaeuser's mill at Valliant is the largest paper mill in the United States. Weyerhaeuser engages in high-yield forestry, which uses clear-cutting to take all the trees at a time. Once the area is cleared, it is contoured and replanted with an average of 900 seedlings per acre.

The Choctaw and Chickasaw nations included all of southern Oklahoma south of the Canadian River. Later, in 1855, the Choctaw and Chickasaw separated, with the Choctaws receiving the eastern portion of southern Oklahoma and the Chickasaws the western half. The Choctaw Nation was divided into three districts—Moshulatubbee, Pushmataha and Okla Falaya or Apukshunnubbee. Okla Falaya was east of the Kiamichi River and west of the Arkansas border. Pushmataha occupied that region west of the Kiamichi River and the Moshulatubbee District and ran west for al-

Right: Sunset on the rock-strewn shore of 89,000-acre Lake Texoma along the border between Oklahoma and Texas.

Facing Page: Honey Creek spilling over the remnants of the once mighty Arbuckle Mountains, now a low range of eroded limestone hills covered with red cedar, blackjacks, and scrub oaks. STEVE MULLIGAN

most 120 miles. Each district was given a district capital and divided into counties.

Skullyville, Moshulatubbee's seat, was founded in 1831 as the site of the Choctaw Agency. Before its destruction during the Civil War by Union troops, it was the site of the annual annuity payments to the Choctaw. In 1844 the New Hope School for Choctaw girls was opened at Skullyville. Conser, also in LeFlore County, was the home of Peter Conser, a prominent Choctaw light-horseman, who headed the tribe's law enforcement organization. Summerville, in LeFlore County, was the location of the Sugar Loaf County Court House.

West of Skullyville and south of Sallisaw is the Robert S. Kerr Reservoir. This 42,000-acre lake is an important part of the Arkansas River Navigation Project. Along its southern shore is the Sequoyah Wildlife Refuge.

Four miles north of Skullyville was Fort Coffee, established in June 1834 to protect the nearby Choctaw Agency. In November of 1838, federal troops abandoned the post. In 1843, the site was transformed into Fort Coffee Academy for Choctaw boys by the Methodist Church. During the Civil War, the post was reoccupied by Confederate forces until 1863 when it was burned by Union troops.

To the south of Skullyville is Lake Wister, a 4,000-acre reservoir on the Poteau River. South of Wister, near Fanshawe, is a 16,316-acre public hunting area stretching along the Fourche Maline arm of Lake Wister. Poteau, along the west shore of Lake Wister, is located between Suger Loaf and Cavanal mountains, two of the highest peaks in the Ouachitas. It is the home of the Robert S. Kerr Museum.

Apukshunnubbee District's capital at Alikchi, in present-day McCurtain County, was established in 1850. Meaning "to doctor," the name comes from nearby Sulphur Spring, a well-known health spa. In July of 1899, William Going was the last person executed under Choctaw law. As was the custom, after being found guilty, Going was allowed to return to his home to put his affairs in order, after giving his word that he would return on the execution date. On the

date prescribed he returned to Alikchi and was shot to death.

Eagle, Eagle Town or Eagletown, near Bethabara Crossing on the Mountain Fork River, was a major government ration station for the Choctaw and considered the end of their Trail of Tears. At the site is a 2,000-year-old cypress tree with a circumference of 45 feet. In 1832 Bethabara Mission was opened at Eagletown. It served as the council grounds for Eagle County. In addition to a log court house, a pin oak "whipping tree" stood in the center of the grounds. Offenders were bound to the tree to receive lashing for violations of tribal law. Eagletown's Stockbridge Mission dates back to 1837 and was founded by Reverend Cyrus Byington, who compiled the *Dictionary of the Choctaw Language*.

One of the earliest settlements in the region was at Millerton, which was the seat of Miller County, Arkansas. This was the result of an inaccurate survey that granted the extreme eastern portion of present-day Oklahoma to Arkansas before the correct boundary was drawn. Northeast of Millerton is Wheelock Academy, opened in 1832 by Alfred Wright, who translated the Choctaw language into writing. Nearby Wheelock Presbyterian Church was founded in 1842 and is the oldest continuously-operating church in the state.

Fort Towson was established in May 1824 to guard the southern border of the United States, which then was the Red River. The post was abandoned in 1829. With the removal of the Choctaw, however, it was reoccupied. Fort Towson also served as the seat of Towson County, Choctaw Nation. It was deactivated in 1854, but reoccupied by Confederate troops during the Civil War.

Antlers, originally called Beaver's Station, was the site of the Battle of Antlers in March of 1893 over the disputed Choctaw tribal election of 1892. Silas Lewis, a member of the Nationalist Party, was sentenced to death for his part in the uprising. Sent home to arrange his affairs, on the day of his execution he returned to the court house and calmly sat down before the oak tree used as a whipping post to await his death by firing squad.

Goodland, the home of Goodland Presbyterian Mission, School and Children's Home, was founded in 1848. It is one of the oldest Protestant Indian orphanages in the nation. The present-day seat of Choctaw County is Hugo, east of Goodland. Hugo is best known as a circus town and once was the winter home of the Al G. Kelley & Miller Bros., George W. Cole and Tex Carson circuses. The local Mount Olive Cemetery has a special section, Showmen's Rest, dedicated to circus performers.

Caddo, in present-day Bryan County, was the largest cotton market in Indian Territory, and the second-largest town in population in the 1870s. To the southwest was Fort McCulloch, established by Confederate Brigadier General Albert Pike in March 1862. The fort was abandoned in July 1862, but later was reoccupied by pro-Southern Indian troops. West of Fort McCulloch was Fort Washita, established in 1842 as a buffer between the Plains Indians and the Five Tribes. The post was seized by Confederate forces in May 1861. Impressive ruins remain of the huge stone buildings.

The Choctaws, who produced the first written constitution in the state on June 3, 1834, had four capitals. The first capital was west of Tuskahoma at Nunih Waya, named after the Choctaw's sacred mound in Mississippi. Doaksville, next to Fort Towson, was the tribe's capital from 1850 to 1863. Founded by the Doaks brothers, who opened a fur trading post at the site in 1824, Doaksville was a major port for steamboats plying the Red River, and had two girls schools, Goodwater, opened in 1837, and Pine Ridge, opened in 1845.

Doaksville also was the center of Robert M.

Jones's far-reaching cotton plantations. Jones, probably the richest man in Indian Territory prior to the Civil War, maintained his home at Rose Hill, west of Doaksville. Elaborately finished in oak, maple, walnut and mahogany, the house was filled with French furniture. Jones owned 500 slaves, who maintained six plantations—Lake West, Boggy, Rose Hill, Root Hog, Shawneetown and Walnut Bayou. His cotton crop was so extensive that he operated two steamboats to carry the crop to markets in New Orleans. It was at Jones's Rose Hill Plantation that Confederate Brigadier General Stand Watie surrendered on June 25, 1865, thereby becoming the last Southern general to do so. Another large cotton plantation was maintained by Samuel Garland at Janis in McCurtain County.

Boggy Depot started as a payment center for Choctaw annuities in 1837, and for a short time in 1858 it served as the Choctaw capital. At Boggy Depot in 1872 the Reverend J.S. Murrow started one of the first Masonic Lodges in what was to become Oklahoma. The town was the home of the Reverend Allen Wright, Principal Chief of the Choctaws, and the originator of the name Oklahoma.

The main Confederate commissary depot in Indian Territory was located nearby, at today's Boggy Depot Recreation Area. The local Presbyterian Church served as a military hospital. Boggy Depot's strategic importance was dictated by its position on the Texas Road, the main north-south route through Oklahoma, and its closeness to the Butterfield Overland Stage Route. The Texas Road was so well-established that when United States Highway 69 was constructed it basically followed its trail.

Opened by John Butterfield in 1858 to provide semiweekly mail service between the Mississippi River and California, the Butterfield Overland Stage Route crossed 192 miles of Indian Territory from Fort Smith to Colbert's Ferry. Under Choctaw law the route through Indian Territory was maintained by local residents, who in turn were allowed to charge for its usage. Fees ranged from 50¢ for a four-wheeled vehicle drawn by four or more animals to 1¢ per head for cattle, horses, mules, hogs or sheep. In the Chickasaw Nation, B.F. Colbert was licensed to maintain a ferry across the Red River and to charge a $1.50 fee for each four-horse wagon.

From 1861 to 1883 the Choctaw capital was at Chahta Tamaha, Choctaw Town or Armstrong, east of Bokchito. The community was established in 1844 by the Baptists as the Armstrong Male Academy for Choctaws. Closed during the Civil War, it was reopened in 1882 by the Presbyterians. Here representatives of the Cherokee, Choctaw, Chickasaw, Creek, Seminole and Caddo formed the United United Nations of Indian Territory of Indian Territory.

Northeast of Armstrong is Durant, the seat of Bryan County. Named for the prominent Choctaw, Dickson

Above: *The remains of the West Barracks of Fort Washita. Constructed of locally quarried limestone, the post was built in 1843 by General Zachery Taylor to separate the Five Tribes from the Plains Indians.*
Left: *Travertine stone forms Turner Falls, deep in the Arbuckle Mountains.*

Durant, the community is the home of Southeastern Oklahoma State University. Known as the "City of Magnolias," its most famous son was Oklahoma governor Robert L. Williams, whose papers are maintained by the Durant City Library.

In 1883, the Choctaw capital was returned to Tuskahoma, near Nunih Waya, and a large two-story wood and brick council house was erected. Tuskahoma remained the capital of the Choctaw Nation until tribal governments ended with Oklahoma's statehood. Tuskahoma also was the site of the Tuskahoma Female Academy that opened in 1891 as a companion to the Jones Male Academy in Hartshorne.

Like the Choctaw Nation, the Chickasaw divided their nation into counties—Panola, Pontotoc, Tishomingo and Pickens. All of Panola and Tishomingo counties, the eastern third of Pickens County and the eastern half of Pontotoc County were in southeastern Oklahoma. The Chickasaw national capital was at Tishomingo, originally known as Good Springs. Jack-

son Frazier built the first home in the community in 1850, and the following year the Chickasaw Manual Labor School was opened on nearby Sand Creek. Chickasaw affairs were directed from a log cabin capitol until 1856 when the building burned. Two years later a large brick capitol building was completed. It burned in 1890 and a third capitol was constructed. This imposing native granite structure became the court house of Johnston County at statehood. Today the structure is maintained as the Choctaw tribal center and cultural museum.

North of Tishomingo is Devil's Den on Pennington Creek. The unique geological formation is formed by the overhang of two huge rocks in the midst of a rugged boulder-strewn area. An early-day outlaw hideout, the region contains such geological features as the Devil's Chair, Dead Man's Cave, the Devil's Coffin, the Witch's Tomb and Bullet Prairie.

Also along the banks of Pennington Creek is the Tishomingo National Fish Hatchery, one of the largest fish hatcheries in the United States. Southeast of Tishomingo is the 16,600-acre Tishomingo National Wildlife Refuge and northeast of the community is the Blue River Public Fishing and Hunting area.

In the extreme northwestern corner of old Tishomingo County is present-day Sulphur. Well-known for its mineral water spas, Sulphur's medicinal springs attracted thousands of visitors annually as early as the pre-Civil War period. There are 31 large mineral springs in the region, including Pavilion Springs and Antelope Springs. In 1902, the Chickasaw Nation transferred title of the spas to the federal government to create Platt National Park, and the springs became the center of a thriving tourist industry. The park later was renamed the Chickasaw National Recreational Area.

Medicinal spas and springs were common in southeastern Oklahoma. Bromide, also known as Juanita or Zenobia, with several medicinal springs gave rise to a number of spas. Kosoma, in Pushmataha County, was famous for its medicinal sulphur springs.

In answer to Chickasaw complaints about raids by the Plains tribes, Fort Arbuckle was built on Wild Horse Creek in southeastern Garvin County in 1852. In May 1861 the post was occupied by Texas troops. Reoccupied by federal forces after the Civil War, the post was abandoned permanently in 1870. Initial Point, east of Fort Arbuckle, is the spot from which all modern surveys of Oklahoma, with the exception of the Panhandle, are made.

Pontotoc County's seat was at Stonewall, with the Collins Institute and the Chickasaw National Academy nearby. One of the largest communities in old Pontotoc County is Ada, the present-day seat of Pontotoc County and headquarters for the Chickasaw Nation. Ada was a wide-open town during its early years, with a reported 36 murders in 1908. Eventually local residents took matters into their own hands and, in 1909, hanged four accused murderers, the largest lynching ever to take place in the state. Ada is also the home of East Central Oklahoma State University. At the entrance to the school's campus is a 350-million-year-old fossilized callixylon.

The Creek Nation, in southeastern Oklahoma north of the Canadian River, was divided into six districts—Coweta, Okmulgee, Muskogee, Deep Fork, Eufaula and Wewoka. Portions of two, Eufaula and Deep Fork, and most of Wewoka were in southeastern Oklahoma. Eufaula was the court house for the Eufaula District. To the east was North Fork Town, which stood at the junction of the California and Texas roads. In 1872, North Fork Town was moved one and a half miles west and renamed Eufaula.

Northeast of Eufaula was the site of Asbury Mission and Manual Labor School. In 1859 delegates from the Seminole, Creek, Choctaw, Chickasaw and Cherokee nations adopted the Asbury Mission Compact, the beginning of the movement for an all-Indian state. East of Eufaula is Eufaula Dam, which forms Eufaula Reservoir. This 102,500-acre lake is the largest in the state and sprawls along 600 miles of shoreline.

Wetumka, southwest of Eufaula, is the spiritual center of the Creeks who brought the tribe's sacred fire with them over the Trail of Tears. North of Wetumka is Thlopthlocco Church, which still holds services in the Muscogee language. North of Wetumka is Weleetka, another Creek settlement, and fifteen miles west of Weleetka is the Old Hickory Stomp Grounds, the center of the Crazy Snake Rebellion of 1901—the last "Indian uprising" in the American West.

The Seminole Nation was the other Indian tribe to occupy portions of southeastern Oklahoma. To serve the tribe, an agency was located east of Tribbey. Following the Civil War, the Seminole domain, which originally included all the land west of the Creek Nation between the Canadian and the North Fork of the Canadian rivers, was reduced drastically. Council Town, in Pottawatomie County, was the first Seminole capital, but in 1867 it was moved to Wewoka. Unfortunately, the survey dividing the Creek and Seminole was in error, and a portion of Wewoka actually was in the Creek Nation. The true boundary between the two nations is Seminole Street, a half block east of Wewoka's Main Street. A pecan tree, standing on the square in Wewoka, served as the whipping tree to punish violators of tribal law.

Wewoka Mission north of Wewoka was established by the Presbyterians as a boarding school for Seminole girls. In an effort to upgrade tribal education, two educational institutions—Mekasukey Academy for Boys and Emhaka Academy for Girls—were built by the Seminole Nation in the 1890s, at a cost of $65,000. Another female school, Amahaka Mission, was established in 1894 west of Holdenville. One of the school's early superintendents was Alice Brown Davis, who later became the first female to be chosen chief of the Seminole.

In the 1920s the Seminole Nation was the site of one of the largest oil discoveries ever made in America—the Greater Seminole Oil Field, which covers almost 1,300 square miles. Production in the area began in 1902; however, the heyday of the region began with the completion of the Betsy Foster No. 1, near Wewoka, in March 1923. The St. Louis Oil Field produced almost 173 million barrels of oil by 1950. It was discovered by the Darby Petroleum Company and the Independent Oil and Gas Company, north of the town of St. Louis in 1926. In the same year, the Seminole City Field was located by the Indian Territory Illuminating Oil Company (ITIO) east of the town of Seminole.

By 1950, the Earlsboro Field's cumulative production stood at almost 132 million barrels of crude. It was

Members of the Chickasaw Lighthorse guarding a shipment of $100,000 being hauled from Ravia to Tishomingo as payment to the Chickasaws.

located in March 1926 when the Morgan and Flynn Oil Company completed the Ingram No. 1 along the Pottawatomie-Seminole county line near Earlsboro. The Bowlegs Field was opened in June of 1926, but its huge output did not start until the ITIO tapped the Wilcox sand in January 1927. By 1950 the Bowlegs Field had produced over 130 million barrels of oil. The Little River Field was located by ITIO along the banks of Salt Creek in July 1927 and produced more than 123 million barrels of oil by 1950.

The Greater Seminole Field gave rise to the town of Cromwell, one of the state's "wickedest" oil boom settlements. It was in Cromwell that legendary lawman Bill Tillman was gunned down. Among other Seminole oil booms towns were Saswaka, Bowlegs, Earlsboro and Maud. The Walker Camp, operated by ITIO near Bowlegs, was a model oil-field community.

Seminole, the seat of Seminole County, became the focal point of the Seminole Field. In 1907 Seminole had a population of only 700; however, with the discovery of oil the community's population jumped to 35,000. With lawmen outnumbered by the gamblers, bootleggers, prostitutes and other camp followers, Seminole mushroomed into a wild oil boom town. Jake Simms, the police chief of Seminole, preserved law and order by painting a wide white stripe across Main Street. Gamblers, prostitutes and bootleggers were kept in Bishop's Alley—north of the white stripe and outside the city limits—plying their trade in such establishments as the Palace, the Big C and the 49ers Dance Hall. More "respectable" citizens lived on the other side of the line. Once, when the *Daily Oklahoman* criticized his policies, Simms stopped the local train, removed all copies of the newspaper and burned them on the community's Main Street.

Following the Reconstruction Treaties of 1866, the Potawatomi and Shawnees were settled in the western part of the Seminole Nation, east of the Unassigned Lands. Shawnee began in the 1870s as Shawneetown on the West Shawnee Cattle Trail, and became the site of the Shawnee Agency. Modern Shawnee started two decades later in 1892 when the Potawatomi lands were opened to homesteaders. Shawnee is the home of St. Gregory's College and Oklahoma Baptist University.

Sacred Heart Mission, founded in 1876, is considered the "Cradle of Oklahoma Catholicism." The mission contained a three-story 50-room monastery, as well as a stone bakery. St. Mary's Academy for Indian Girls operated at Sacred Heart from 1884 to 1943. Sacred Heart was the home of Father Gregory Gerrer, whose painting of Pope Pius X was hung in the Vatican in 1904.

Shawnee's great rival was Tecumseh, which was founded in 1891 and named the seat of Pottawatomie County, Oklahoma Territory, a position that was reaffirmed by the Constitutional Convention in 1907. In 1909 the seat was moved to Shawnee, but four years later it was returned to Tecumseh. The controversy was not settled until 1930 when the county seat was moved permanently to Shawnee.

Southeastern Oklahoma has a strong tie to the Old South and often is called "Little Dixie," and is more akin to the South than to the higher, drier western part of the state. This association can be traced to the removal of the Choctaws, Cherokees, Chickasaws, Creeks and Seminole to the area. With them came Southern traditions and a cotton culture. Plantations were developed, antebellum mansions built and the Southern culture was transplanted into southeastern Oklahoma. Non-Indian migrations into the region also tend to originate predominately from the Old South. The area is also rich in natural beauty and scenery. Its legacy as "Little Dixie" has created a unique cultural identity that it has maintained for decades and which gives the region a charm that has remained distinct throughout its history.

Above: *The Quartermaster Depot in historic Fort Reno. Established in 1874, the post served to protect the Cheyenne-Arapaho Agency at Darlington and keep watch over the reservation.*

Facing page: *The opening of the Unassigned Lands on April 22, 1889, as depicted in this mural by Charles Banks Wilson, in the State Capitol.*

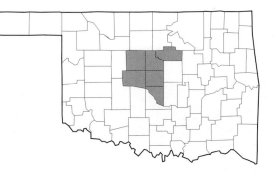

THE UNASSIGNED LANDS
CENTRAL OKLAHOMA

With the establishment of the Plains Indian reservations in Oklahoma, a large portion of central Oklahoma was left vacant. Although it had been removed from the jurisdiction of the Five Tribes, it had not been assigned to any other tribe. This 1,887,796.47-acre area was known as the Unassigned Lands and included all of present-day Payne, Logan, Kingfisher and Cleveland counties and most of Canadian and Oklahoma counties.

This huge expanse of unoccupied territory quickly attracted the attention of homesteaders, and between 1873 and 1879 six bills were introduced calling for the organization of the region as Oklahoma Territory. Called Boomers, several groups, including James M. Bell's Indian Territory Colonization Society and Charles Carpenter, who led several abortive colonies into the Unassigned Lands, insisted the area already was a part of the public domain and therefore open to homesteaders.

In August 1879, David L. Payne assumed the leadership of the Boomer movement. He organized and served as president of the Oklahoma Colony, which offered members a 160-acre homestead in the Unassigned Lands in exchange for a $2 membership fee. Payne led a total of ten ill-fated invasions between 1880 and 1884. His first crossed into Indian Territory on April 26, 1880, and for six days drove south to the valley of the Canadian River, about one mile from downtown Oklahoma City. Calling the settlement New Philadelphia, Payne's followers spent three days laying out claims and a townsite. Discovered by federal troops, Payne and his followers were taken to Fort Reno. Although he hoped to be tried in federal court and thus have the judiciary rule

JOHN ELK III

on the opening of the Unassigned Lands, Payne's plans were thwarted when he was escorted back to Kansas and released.

Payne launched a second invasion in July 1880; however, he again was detained. Payne told the military that it was illegal for troops to arrest civilians for longer than five days and asked that he be taken before Judge Issac Parker in Fort Smith, Arkansas. Judge Parker scheduled the case for November 1880 and released Payne, but the charges were dropped.

Payne led other homesteaders into the Unassigned Lands twice in 1881, only to be expelled. In February 1883 Payne's Boomers established Camp Alice, west of Arcadia, before being removed. In August 1883 another invasion took place, this time without Payne. Although he was not with the invaders, Payne nonetheless was arrested. He was found inside Indian Territory again in August 1884. He was arrested, taken to Fort Smith, released, and then indicted again. Before his trial, however, he died, in November 1884.

Payne's place was taken by William L. Couch,

Right: Hell's Half Acre in Guthrie on May 26, 1889, shortly after the Run of '89. The confusion in forming city governments where none previously existed led to political chaos in many Oklahoma Territory communities that literally were "born overnight."

Facing page: A group of Boomers led by David L. Payne at Camp Alice west of present-day Arcadia in March of 1883.

who led three hundred homesteaders to present-day Stillwater in December 1884, only to be driven back to Kansas by troops. Couch made another invasion the following October. This time he established a settlement at Council Grove, in western Oklahoma City; however, it quickly was discovered and the settlers evicted.

Finally, in February 1889, Congress passed legislation opening the Unassigned Lands; on March 23, 1889, President Benjamin Harrison issued a proclamation announcing that the opening would take place at noon on April 22, 1889. The disposition of homesteads was to be made by a run. The lands were surveyed and mounds of stones marked each quarter section.

Some estimates placed the number of hopeful homesteaders at 50,000. They were competing for 11,797 homesteads. Those making the run did so on foot, horseback, muleback, in wagons, carts, buggies, surreys, sulkies, buckboards, and even on bicycles. In addition, others sought places on special trains that were to enter the Unassigned Lands from the north and south boundaries. There also were a number of "Sooners," who crossed the line before noon and, after hiding in the underbrush, sprang out at the appointed hour to stake a claim.

By nightfall on Monday, April 22, the Unassigned Lands were settled. Several communities literally were born grown. Guthrie, Oklahoma Station, Kingfisher and Norman were tent cities that evening. Stillwater was not established for several more weeks. Although the land had been opened, it was not until the Organic Act creating Oklahoma Territory was passed by Congress—May 2, 1890—that permanent town governments and counties were organized. The Organic Act also added the Panhandle to the Unassigned Lands to form Oklahoma Territory. Guthrie was named the territorial capital and seven counties, numbered one through seven, were established. Six were in the Unassigned Lands: Logan, Oklahoma, Norman, Canadian, Kingfisher and Payne.

Guthrie, a depot on the Atchison, Topeka and Santa Fe Railroad and the site of one of two land offices where homesteaders could register their claims, attracted the greatest number of settlers, with an estimated 15,000 settlers staking town lots. Federal law prohibited townsites in excess of 320 acres, but Guthrie's early developers eluded the provision by plotting four half-section townsites—Guthrie, East Guthrie, West Guthrie and Capitol Hill.

On the evening of April 22 a gathering was held to discuss a provisional municipal government for Guthrie. Afterward, three names were presented for consideration for mayor. To determine the winner, a wagon was provided for each nominee and voters formed lines before each wagon. Those in line then were counted; however, because many of the men switched lines, or changed places so that they could be counted twice, the first election was voided.

On April 24, one of the candidates withdrew and the remaining two agreed to name three representatives. These six men would choose a seventh member for a selection committee; they named B.V. Dyer mayor on April 25. Once the mayor was chosen the other municipal offices were filled. East Guthrie, West Guthrie and Capitol Hill followed suit, but with the passage of the Organic Act on May 2, 1890, Guthrie and the other three communities were united.

Guthrie became the dominant community of the new territory. Numerous ornate brick Victorian homes were built along its tree-line avenues. Its turn-of-the-century atmosphere has been preserved, and much of

downtown and the adjoining residential areas have been designated a Historic District by the National Park Service. During the Christmas season, Guthrie is lit by tens of thousands of colored bulbs as the community re-creates a "territorial Christmas." Many of its Victorian buildings have been restored, including the Harrison House and the Stone Lion Inn. The nationally-acclaimed architect Joseph Foucart designed many of Guthrie's early buildings, including the Rice House and the Bonfils Building. The Victor Building's Sand Plum Restaurant and the Pollard Theater are two of the community's best-known attractions.

Among Guthrie's other attractions is the first Carnegie Library in Oklahoma, and the State Capital Publishing Museum, former home of the Cooperative Publishing Company, the territory's first daily newspaper, the *State Capital*. Guthrie also attracted a number of political activists like Carry Nation, the leader of the prohibition movement who first published her anti-liquor, anti-tobacco and anti-Masonic newspaper, *The Hatchet*, at Guthrie in June 1905. Cora V. Diehl, the first woman elected to office in Oklahoma, was also a local resident, as was William Wrigley, who produced his first chewing gum at his office on North Division Street.

Because Oklahoma Territory was "wet," Guthrie boasted numerous saloons. Tom Mix, the cowboy movie star of the 1920s, once worked at the Blue Belle Saloon and brothel, which has been restored, as has the old federal jail.

Although Guthrie was named the territorial capital, as early as 1890 legislation was introduced to move it to Oklahoma City or Kingfisher. In 1892, Congress ended the fight and reaffirmed Guthrie as the territorial capital; two years later Congress provided that should the capital be moved, territorial officials would forfeit their salaries. Nevertheless the debate continued.

Because of the controversy, neither territorial nor state officials built permanent capitol buildings in Guthrie, although ten acres had been set aside on Capitol Hill for the capitol's location and $100,000 promised for construction. Instead, the various offices were housed in a number of buildings: The Avon Building served as the first state governor's office; the three-story City Hall on West Oklahoma Avenue, completed in 1902, served as the unofficial capitol. In 1907, Guthrie officials built a convention hall on Capitol Hill. City officials planned to loan it to the state as the home of the state legislature.

Guthrie was called the "Capital of Oklahoma Masonry," and in 1898 work on one of the world's largest Masonic structures was begun on a ten-acre site. The $2.5 million Greek Doric structure was designed by J.O. Parr and contained a 3,500-seat auditorium, a 62-foot-wide, 90-foot-deep stage, and a 1,500-seat dining hall. In addition, Guthrie was the home of the Masonic Home for the Aged, the Masonic Home for Children, and the Grand Lodge Temple.

The Run of '89 gave birth to several other Logan County communities. The most important was Langston, an all-black community established by E.P. McCabe. Langston was the site of the Langston University, an all-black university established in 1897. Unfortunately, Langston did not prosper and many early residents moved to Guthrie; McCabe was among them.

El Reno, the county seat of Canadian County, was founded in 1889, on the south side of the North Fork of the Canadian River near the western border of the Unassigned Lands. There were two other nearby communities—Frisco and Reno City. At first it appeared Reno City would be the premier community as it was on the route surveyed by the Chicago, Rock Island and Pacific Railroad. But when the developers of Reno City refused to give the railroad half of the town's lots, the railroad was rerouted through El Reno. Disappointed, many residents of Reno City placed their

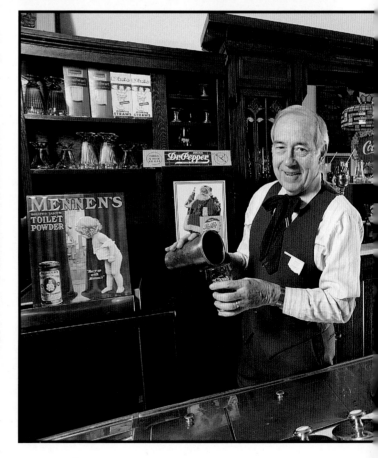

Above: *Country fun in Norman.*
Left: *A Victorian-era drugstore museum highlights the National Historic Preservation District in Guthrie.*

Facing page, top: *The '89er Day Parade through Guthrie. The annual event attracts thousands of onlookers.*
Bottom: *The State Capital Publishing Company in Guthrie. The restored territorial-era establishment is maintained as an historic site by the Oklahoma Historical Society. It was here that Frank Greer published the* Oklahoma State Capital *newspaper. Greer's scathing indictments of the Democrat-controlled legislature helped prompt the solons to move the state capital to Oklahoma City in 1910.*

JIM ARGO

businesses and homes on wooden skids and dragged them to El Reno. Likewise, Frisco disappeared after the Choctaw, Oklahoma and Gulf Railroad bypassed it in favor of Yukon.

Being at the intersection of major east-west and north-south railroad lines, El Reno quickly grew. Its growth was enhanced as the Chicago, Rock Island and Pacific made it a major division center. When the Cheyenne-Arapaho and Wichita-Caddo reservations were opened in 1901, El Reno was one of two sites selected as a district land office. More than 150,000 people

doned, but in April of that same year it was reoccupied as a remount station. During World War II the post served as a POW camp for German soldiers and remained in service until 1948, when it was taken over by the Department of Agriculture as the Fort Reno Livestock Research Station. Many of the old buildings remain.

Kingfisher had existed prior to the Run of '89 as a stage stand operated by King Fisher. When the run started at noon on April 22, not all the participants entered the Unassigned Lands from the northern or

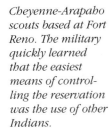

Cheyenne-Arapaho scouts based at Fort Reno. The military quickly learned that the easiest means of controlling the reservation was the use of other Indians.

crowded into El Reno for the drawing. That part of the Wichita-Caddo Reserve south of the Canadian River was added to Canadian County after the opening.

In 1934 the federal government constructed the nearby United States Reformatory. El Reno is also the location of Redlands Community College. Nearby, the Darlington Indian Agency was established in 1869 for the Cheyenne and Arapaho. In 1879, the *Cheyenne Transporter*, the first newspaper in western Indian Territory, was published at Darlington. In 1897 the Cheyenne Agency was moved to Concho, the home of the Cheyenne and Arapaho Boarding School. The Cheyenne and Arapaho were administered separately until 1909 when Darlington was closed and the two tribes reunited under the Concho Agency. In 1910 the Oklahoma Masons took over Darlington as a orphanage. In 1932 the facilities were converted into the State Game Farm and became one of the world's largest quail hatcheries.

West of El Reno is Fort Reno, established in 1874 to provide protection for Darlington. In April 1875, the Battle of the Sand Hill took place on the south side of the North Fork of the Canadian River, opposite Darlington. In February 1908 Fort Reno was aban-

southern boundary. Several thousand made the dash from the western edge and were called "West Liners," as opposed to the "North Liners" or "South Liners." Because King Fisher's stage station was just east of the 98th meridian, the west boundary of the Unassigned Lands, it was the goal of many of the West Liners.

Within an hour of the opening, almost 2,500 homesteaders had claimed all the lots around King Fisher's station, which they named Lisbon. Because they were farther away, it was not until almost 3:00 P.M. that the North Liners arrived. With all available lots already chosen, they established another 160-acre townsite north of Lisbon that they named Kingfisher City.

In an effort to end the confusion resulting from two townsites, members of the International Order of the Odd Fellows and the Grand Army of the Republic called for a meeting to organize a single municipal government; nothing was accomplished, and on April 28 a temporary government was established for Lisbon. Lisbon's early civic leaders concerned themselves primarily with regulating gambling by establishing weekly fees of $5 for draw poker and Chuck-a-Luck tables and $15 for stud poker tables.

Residents of Kingfisher City also formed a municipal government. In July 1889, however, the Post Office Department dropped Lisbon and named Kingfisher as the local post office, and with the passage of the Organic Act of 1890, the two communities were merged.

In 1893 Kingfisher was the site of the organization of the Oklahoma Territorial Press Association, forerunner of the Oklahoma Press Association and the Oklahoma Historical Society, and in 1898 the community hosted the organizational meeting of the Negro Teachers Association of Oklahoma Territory. Kingfisher also was the home of Oklahoma Territorial Governor Abraham J. Seay. His three-story mansion and the nearby Chisholm Trail Museum are open to the public. Kingfisher's economy boomed again in the post-World War II era with the discovery of the nearby Sooner Trend Oil Field.

The rich farmland of Kingfisher County attracted a number of European immigrants, many of them Germans. They were concentrated in the northwestern part of the county and in 1894 formed the community of Kiel, named for the German city. During World War I, anti-German hysteria reached the point in Oklahoma where the teaching of the German language in schools was prohibited, the making of sauerkraut viewed as disloyal and several German language newspapers were burned by mobs. To demonstrate their loyalty to America, the residents of Kiel changed the name of their town to Loyal. Like Kiel, Okarche was a center of German settlement and once had a German language newspaper.

Hennessey started as Bull Foot Stage Station on the same stage route as Kingfisher's. Founded in 1889, the town was named for Pat Hennessey, who operated a freight line along the stage route. In July 1874, a group of Indians raided and burned Bull Foot station and then caught Hennessey, George Fand, Thomas Caloway and Ed Cook at nearby Buffalo Springs, on the eastern edge of Hennessey. The Indians killed Hennessey and the others and took their supplies. The spot became a well-known landmark on the Chisholm Trail.

Cleveland County marked the southern extension of the Unassigned Lands. Norman began in 1886 as a camp for surveyors marking the route of the Atchison, Topeka and Santa Fe Railroad. The camp was named for Aubrey Norman. When the railroad was built, a section house and switch were built and the location was called Camp Norman or Norman Switch.

When it was announced that the Unassigned Lands would be opened, D.L. Larsh, T.R. Waggoner and Tyler Blake of Purcell formed a townsite company to settle Norman Switch. Boarding the train to make the run, Larsh stepped off at Norman only to discover that a group of railroad engineers already

had platted the town. Fortunately for Larsh, he was able to convince them to turn their claims over to his group. Only about 150 people staked their claims in Norman on April 22 and it was not until May 4 that a provisional municipal government was formed.

In September 1890 the Southern Methodist Church opened High Gate Female College in the community. In 1893 the Oklahoma Sanitarium, to care for the mentally ill, was established in Norman. In 1895 it moved into the buildings formally occupied by High Gate Female College, and in 1915 was acquired by the state and renamed Central State Griffin Memorial Hospital, now the state's major mental health facility.

In 1892 the territorial legislature selected Norman as the site for the University of Oklahoma. Classes started in rented buildings in downtown Norman, but a 285-acre main campus soon was acquired. The University of Oklahoma is one of the nation's outstanding institutions of higher education. One of the country's first schools of petroleum geology was opened on the campus in 1900. Perhaps best known, however, is the school's football team, the Sooners, who had won six NCAA national championships by 1993.

Modern-day Lexington started with the Run of '89. Because the settlement was on the river dividing the Unassigned Lands from Indian Territory, it quickly became a border liquor town supplying whiskey to residents of "dry" Indian Territory. One of the community's best known establishments was the Sand Bar Saloon. Located on a sand bar in the river, it was connected to Indian Territory by a footbridge. Nearby is the 8,613-acre Lexington Public Hunting Area.

One of the last areas to be settled was Stillwater. Although the surrounding region had been claimed by homesteaders, an 80-acre tract along Stillwater Creek remained unoccupied. In May 1890 the Stillwater Townsite Company acquired title to that land and another 180 acres. Town lots sold for $5 and residential lots two for $5. In 1889 a town charter was approved, and in 1891, Stillwater was incorporated.

Stillwater is the location of Oklahoma State University, the state's agricultural and mechanical institution created by the territorial legislature in December 1890 as Oklahoma Agricultural & Mechanical College. Classes started in December 1891, in the local Congregational Church. Old Central, the university's first building, was completed in June of 1894 on the 146-acre main campus. The school's Agricultural Experimental Station was opened in April of 1892. Oklahoma State University's athletic program boasts more NCAA championships than any other university in the nation.

Perkins, south of Stillwater, was the home of United States Deputy Marshall Frank "Pistol Pete" Eaton. Eaton, with his handlebar mustache, cowboy clothes and guns was the model for the Oklahoma State Uni-

J. PAT CARTER/OU/PHOTO SERVICES

Above: The Administration
Building at the University of
Oklahoma in Norman.
Established by the Territorial
Legislature, the University of
Oklahoma opened its doors in
1892 and is the home of the
internationally famous Stovall
Museum.

Right: There's always extra
excitement when the OU
Sooners meet the OSU
Cowboys.

Facing page: The rotunda of
the Oklahoma State Capitol,
which was constructed during
World War I. The shortage of
steel during the war years
prevented the addition of the
planned dome to cap the
structure.

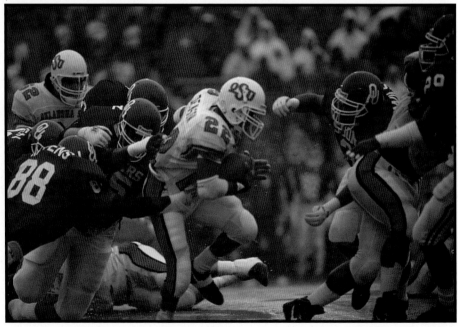

versity mascot. West of Stillwater is Ingalls. It was the site of the 1892 shootout between Bill Doolin, Arkansas Tom Jones, Bob (Bitter Creek) Yokum, Bill Dalton, Dan (Dynamite Dick) Clifton, George Newcomb, Tulsa Jack, Red Buck and other outlaws and deputy marshals E.D. Nix, A.H. Houston, Lafe Shadley, Red Lucas, James Masterson, Dick Speed and others.

Guthrie's primary competition for the location of the capital was Oklahoma City. Prior to 1889, Oklahoma City consisted of a railroad depot and section, post office, boarding house and stage stand. The first legal settlers to arrive were led by Dan Phillips and appeared about 2:00 P.M. on April 22; however, it was reported that within fifteen minutes of the opening members of the Seminole Land and Town Company were laying out streets. Obviously these Sooners had entered the region early so they could be the first to plot the townsite. Surveyors for the Seminole Land and Town Company staked lots along Main Street, while Phillips plotted lots along Reno Avenue. A third townsite company, the Oklahoma Townsite Company, arrived later and surveyed another site south of the railroad depot and organized South Oklahoma. Of the three surveys, Phillips' and the Seminole Land and Town Company's were compatible. But the north-south streets marked by the Oklahoma Townsite Company did not exactly meet the other two, and for many years, streets in downtown Oklahoma City were plagued by jogs.

More than ten thousand people lived in what was to become Oklahoma City at nightfall on April 22. Both Oklahoma Station and South Oklahoma elected mayors and an intense rivalry began. On May 23, 1890, Oklahoma Station elected a provisional municipal government, but approval of a city charter was delayed when Mayor W.L. Couch refused to allow local citizens to vote on the charter and persuaded Captain D.F. Stiles to use federal troops to disperse the unruly mob that gathered to protest. Couch resigned on November 11 and later was shot in a dispute over a homestead claim. With the enactment of the Organic Act, Oklahoma Station and South Oklahoma were combined into the city of Oklahoma and a permanent municipal government was elected in August 1890. Yet the post office was not changed to Oklahoma City until 1923.

Almost immediately, Oklahoma City's leaders began to agitate for the removal of the capital, but it remained in Guthire until 1910 due to national politics. As long as republicans controlled Congress and Oklahoma remained a territory, Guthrie's strong republican faction managed to stop any attempt to move the capital. Statehood, however, ended congressional control.

The Enabling Act, joining Oklahoma and Indian Territory into the State of Oklahoma, specified that the capital would remain in Guthrie until 1913. However, Republican influence waned as Democrats controlled the legislature. Frank Greer, publisher of the *State Capital* and the champion of the Republican Party, attacked the democrat officials almost daily. As the attacks increased, support for Guthrie declined among the legislative leadership. In 1909, an initiative petition, prepared by W.A. Ledbetter, was circulated calling for an election to determine the permanent state capital and allowing any city that submitted a petition with 5,000 names to be placed on the ballot.

Three communities met the requirements—Guthrie, Shawnee and Oklahoma City—and in March 1910 Governor Charles N. Haskell set July 11 as the election date. The vote was 96,488 for Oklahoma City, 31,031 for Guthrie and 8,382 for Shawnee. Haskell, who was in Tulsa when the votes were counted, immediately telegraphed his secretary, W.B. Anthony, telling him to move the state seal to Oklahoma City. Haskell also made arrangements for a special train to carry him to the new capital. Anthony met Haskell at the Lee-Huckins Hotel in downtown Oklahoma City about 6:00 A.M., June 12. Haskell printed "Oklahoma City the capital of the State of Oklahoma" on a piece of hotel stationery, signed and sealed the proclamation. Another hand-printed sign stating "Governor's Office" was place on Haskell's hotel room door.

Guthrie supporters appealed to the Oklahoma Supreme Court, and for several months some state offices remained in Guthrie. In November the court ruled that the election was void. In response, a special session of the legislature named Oklahoma City the state's permanent capital, an act upheld by the State Supreme Court. Although Guthrie's supporters took their fight to the United States Supreme Court, the court ruled that a state had the right to determine the location of its capital, the Enabling Act notwithstanding.

Work on a state capitol building was started in 1914 and completed in 1917. Designed by Sol Layton, the massive limestone and granite building was constructed in the form of a cross. The planned dome for the building was never completed because of the shortage of steel caused by World War I. In 1928 a nearby governor's mansion was completed.

With the acquisition of the state capital, Oklahoma City quickly became the economic center of the state. Economic security was increased by the establishment of the Stockyards City, which became a major cattle and hog market, and the discovery of the prolific Oklahoma City Oil Field, the fourth-largest field in American prior to 1950.

Completed by the Indian Territory Illuminating Oil Company and the Foster Petroleum Company, the Oklahoma City No. 1, just north of the Oklahoma-Cleveland county line, blew in on the Celia Hall lease

Four Boomers arrested by the military during one of their excursions into the Unassigned Lands prior to the Run of '89. They had been captured by Cheyenne-Arapaho scouts from Fort Reno.

in December 1929. The field was characterized by extremely high natural-gas pressure, which resulted in a number of wild wells, the most famous being the Wild Mary Sudik. So great was the production of the Oklahoma City Field that the oil market busted and Governor William A. "Alfalfa Bill" Murray ordered the National Guard into the field, in 1931 and 1933, to shut down the wells and increase the price of oil. Finally, the state legislature passed the Oklahoma Oil Code that eliminated much of the waste.

As the wells moved into residential areas of the community, it was not uncommon for houses to be cut in half to make room for derricks. The cry for control resulted in the passage of U-7 Drilling Zones to protect homeowners and regulate oil field activity. In 1936, the National Guard again was ordered into the Oklahoma City Field to protect drilling on the State Capitol grounds from interference by Oklahoma City officials.

The modern Oklahoma City's metropolitan area includes The Village, Nichols Hills, Warr Acres, Bethany, Spencer, Nicoma Park, Yukon, Choctaw, Edmond, and Midwest City and Del City, which surround Tinker Air Force Base and Logistics Center. The community boasts a number of educational institutions—Oklahoma City University, Rose State Community College, Oklahoma State University in Oklahoma City, Oklahoma City Community College and Southern Nazarene University. There is a wide variety of recreational and cultural attractions, including the Kirkpatrick Center, the National Cowboy Hall, Ballet Oklahoma, Remington Park, the Oklahoma City Zoo and professional sports. The University of Oklahoma's School of Medicine is the center of a medical complex

that is the largest between Kansas City, Missouri, and Houston, Texas. Oklahoma City also has taken great pains to preserve its rich architectural legacy in such Historic Preservation Districts as Heritage Hills, Crown Heights, Capital-Lincoln Terrace, and others.

Just to the north of Oklahoma City is Edmond. Organized on April 22, 1889, Edmond boasted Oklahoma Territory's first newspaper, the *Edmond Sun*, founded by Milton W. Reynolds, better known by his pen name—Kicking Bird. In 1891, the University of Central Oklahoma was established as the territory's normal school for training teachers. Old North Tower, the university's first building, still stands. In 1958, the Church of Christ moved Oklahoma Christian University of Arts and Science to Edmond. The town's economy received a tremendous boost in 1943 with the discovery of the nearby West Edmond Oil Field. East of Edmond is Lake Arcadia.

The communities of the Unassigned Lands are unique in the state's history. Tent cities simply had sprouted where there had been nothing but virgin prairie the previous day. The Unassigned Lands attracted settlers from throughout the country and from many foreign countries. Likewise, because it was "born grown," there was no transitory period in which the economic or cultural base of a new territory was established. As a result it did not have the distinct Southern culture of Little Dixie, the Native American heritage of Indian Territory, nor the frontier flavor of the Wild West. Instead, it became a blending of many cultures—Western, Midwestern, Southern, Southwestern, Northern and European—a heritage that is reflected in the cultural diversity of the region today.

Above: *Downtown Oklahoma City skyline. On the left is the historic Colcord Building, one of the first high-rise buildings constructed in the community. Rising in the center is the First National Bank and Trust Company building, which at the time of its completion during the Great Depression contained more aluminum than any other structure between the Mississippi River and the West Coast.*

Facing page, top: *The north side of the State Capitol, which is often considered the front of the building; however, the structure was purposely built to face the south as an example of the state's Southern heritage.*
Bottom: *Financed by John and Eleanor Kirkpatrick, the Kirkpatrick Center in Oklahoma City utilizes a hands-on approach to the interpretation of science and history.*

The rich grasslands of No Man's Land were a mecca for Texas cattlemen who moved their herds of Longhorns into the region following the Civil War.

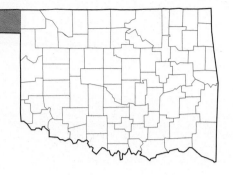

NO MAN'S LAND
THE PANHANDLE

It was not until the Adams-Onis Treaty of 1819 that the boundary between America and Mexico was accurately drawn. Under its provisions the northern border of the Texas Panhandle reached into southern Kansas and Colorado. The following year, the Missouri Compromise banned slavery north of 36°30', the southern border of Missouri, which also is the southern border of the Oklahoma Panhandle. Texas was admitted to the Union as a slave state in 1845, but it was not until the Compromise of 1850 that the present-day state boundaries were drawn. As Texas boundaries were being mapped, it was discovered that a part of the Texas Panhandle was north of 36° 30'. Texas, as a slave state, surrendered that portion. Because the eastern border of New Mexico was located at the 103rd meridian, the southern border of Kansas at the 37th parallel and the western border of Indian Territory at the 100th meridian, a swath of land stretching 34 miles from north to south and 166 miles from east to west—bordering Texas to the north, Kansas to the south, New Mexico to the west and Indian Territory to the east—was not under the jurisdiction of any state or territory. And because its residents were "outside the law," the area became known as "God's Land, but No Man's."

At first there was little interest in No Man's Land and most non-Indian visitors consisted of buffalo hunters. Buffalo hunting became so lucrative that between 1872 and 1874 almost 7 million pounds of buffalo meat were shipped out of No Man's Land to railheads in Kansas and Texas. The bones left by the millions of buffalo slaughtered for their hides and tongues provided an early industry. Settlers gathered the bones and sold them to fertilizer companies. This led to a popular ditty that often was heard in the Panhandle:

Pickin' up bones to keep from starving,
Pickin' up chips to keep from freezing,
Pickin' up courage to keep from leaving,
Way out West in No Man's Land.

Other frequent visitors were travelers along the Cimarron Cutoff of the Santa Fe Trail, which saved ten days on the trip between Missouri and New Mexico. It entered the Panhandle north of Keyes, crossed to the south bank of the Cimarron River and on to Camp Nichols and New Mexico. The ruts, ten feet deep and twenty feet wide, formed by the thousands of wagons traveling the cutoff, can still be seen near Camp Nichols.

Camp Nichols was established in 1865 to protect emigrants on the Santa Fe Trail from Indians. Originally thought to be located in New Mexico, the post actually was in Cimarron County near Mexhoma. A National Historic Landmark, Camp Nichols can be identified by mounds of crumbled stones that mark the walls, barracks and sentry tower. The post was abandoned in 1865 after Kit Carson's military expedition into the area suppressed the Indian depredations. Another well-known spot on the cutoff was nearby Wheeless Post Office near Camp Nichols. Nearby Hallock Park is composed of 10,000 acres of canyons walls covered by Indian pictographs, mesas and more than 120 springs providing a well-watered campground.

For almost a quarter of a century No Man's Land attracted few permanent residents; however, during the heyday of the range cattle industry Texas stockmen pushed into the region, especially as much of the rangeland in Texas was grazed bare. Many of these early stockmen were displaced Confederate veterans who had lost everything in the Civil War. One such Panhandle pioneer was John Noble Gunn, who, prior to the Civil War, had operated a profitable hemp farm in Randolph County, Missouri. At the outbreak of the fighting, Gunn enlisted in J.O. Shelby's Missouri Confederate Cavalry and served throughout the war. His Confederate sympathy resulted in his family being displaced and his home destroyed. His entire family died as refugees, and when the war ended Gunn headed West and became a cowboy in Texas. Gathering his own herd, Gunn moved into No Man's Land in 1872 and settled along the Sharp's Creek Valley in present-day Texas County.

With no law, no courts and no land offices, Gunn and the other Texas stockmen were able to stake

claims to large tracts of rich grassland. Generally a rancher would settle along a creek and claim all land drained by that creek watershed. Gunn built a native stone house along Sharp's Creek and remarried. Descendants of Gunn, like most of the early pioneers in the region, still own the original family farm, which today is operated by his great-grandsons L.J. Lynch and M.L. Cantrell.

Title to the land remained vague until 1882 when the secretary of the interior ruled that No Man's Land was a part of the public domain. Afterward, the area often was referred to as the Public Land Strip. This pronouncement touched off a rush to the region, and the Beaver City Town Company founded Beaver, which soon became a stop on the Jones and Plummer Cattle Trail.

The trail had been pioneered by C.E. Jones and Joe Plummer in 1874 as a wagon road between the Atchison, Topeka and Santa Fe Railroad at Dodge City, Kansas, and the ranches in the north Texas Panhandle. Local ranchers soon were driving cattle to the railhead at Dodge City along the route. The trail started in the Texas Panhandle and ran north across the

Canadian River to the Oklahoma Panhandle, then northeast to the valley of the Beaver River and on to Kansas, southwest of Dodge City.

These early cattle drives were dominated by longhorns, a cross between Moorish and Mexican cattle. Longhorns were wild, required little, if any, human care, and came in a wide variety of colors—brindle, white, red, orange, dun, yellow, brown, black or any combination. They possessed keen senses of smell, sight, and hearing, and were characterized by a huge set of horns that provided protection from most predators. Longhorns could survive extreme climatic conditions, required little food or water and could walk thousands of miles. The drives were well-organized affairs. Generally, twelve cowboys managed a herd of about 2,500 longhorns. A foreman, or "trail boss," oversaw the drive—a cook and his helper being responsible for feeding the company—while a "horse wrangler" had charge of the remuda, or horse herd. The cowboys usually were paid between $25 and $40 a month.

The drive started at dawn and the animals were allowed to graze on the move for the first couple of

Above: *The rugged terrain of No Man's Land near Kenton. The region once was covered with a 40-foot-thick deposit of volcanic ash.*
Right: *The view from the top of Black Mesa. At 4,972.97 feet above sea level, Black Mesa is the highest point in the state.*

Facing page: *A stormy sunset at Black Mesa. This mesa is the remnant of a prehistoric volcano eruption that sent a 70-foot-thick flow of lava across the land.*

JIM ARGO

hours. A moving herd generally stretched about a mile in length and fifty feet in width at its widest. A regular pace was maintained until noon, when a two-hour halt was called. The drive then resumed until the evening when the cattle were "bedded down" for the night.

Specific stations were maintained by the cowboys. The movement was directed by two men on each side of the head of the herd. Called the "point," they were responsible for maintaining the line of march, negating stampedes and preventing intermingling with other herds. The "swing" and the "flank" were the riders positioned along the sides, responsible for keeping proper spacing. At the rear was the "drag," whose duty was to keep the herd moving and to round up strays. During the night, usually three, two-man shifts watched over the cattle.

Most cowboys were young, mainly teenagers. Twenty percent of them were black and ten percent were Native American. The typical cowboy usually wore heavy woolen trousers and shirts; the shirt sleeves were held up by garters. A large hat offered protection from the elements. A neckerchief was knotted around his neck and could be pulled up to protect the face. Coats were worn in the winter, but a vest was *always* present. In the vest the cowboy could carry a watch, tobacco, or money. Gloves to protect his hands were worn constantly. Boots designed for work on horseback made it awkward to walk on the ground. Heavy leather chaps protected his legs.

It was dangerous work. Broken bones were a constant hazard and a bad fall could cripple or kill. A kick from a horse could be fatal and a stampede might mean being trampled. Fingers often were lost in roping accidents. It was thought that sleeping in the open on the ground often brought on arthritis at an early age. Because of the hazards, dangers and hardships, it is no wonder that the average working life of a cowboy was only seven years.

By the mid-1880s, as many as 30,000 head of cattle were located on No Man's Land ranches. Ranch houses were built, corrals constructed and a thriving range cattle industry was underway. These early-day ranchers, such as Henry C. Hitch, Sr., laid the foundation for a cattle industry that today ranks Texas County first among the state's counties in the number of cattle produced.

The cattle industry changed as the large ranches were established and the glamour of the cowboy was lost. Their days were now filled with hard day-to-day work as cattle had to be tended and fences built. Instead of driving herds north to Kansas, the cowboys found themselves digging post holes, stretching barbed wire and building corrals. There were, however, some advantages. Bunkhouses offered better accommodations than the open ground and the work was more permanent, but the lore and attraction of being a cowboy was beginning to disappear as it was replaced by the modern agribusiness.

Beaver City soon became the "capital" of the Public Land Strip, and by 1887 six thousand settlers lived in the area. Kenton, originally named Carrizo, one of two incorporated towns in Cimarron County, was a booming cattle town known as the "Cowboy Capital of the World." Because of the seasonal influx of young unmarried cowboys, who generally received a portion of their pay at Kenton, the community boasted a number of prosperous saloons offering liquor, women and gambling. In 1907, Kenton was named the seat of Cimarron County, but voters soon moved the government to Boise City.

In an attempt to bring law and order to the region, fifty men gathered in October 1886 and organized a "Claimant's Board" to settle land disputes. Then a petition drive by thirty-four men and one woman called for a meeting to prepare "a code of bylaws." In February 1887 an election was held selecting representatives to a "territorial council" for Cimarron Territory. An elaborate stone plaque in downtown Beaver marks the site of the two-story territorial capitol.

Seven of the nine elected delegates convened in Beaver City in March 1887 and divided No Man's Land into seven counties—Benton, Beaver, Shade, Springer, Turner, Kilgore and Sunset—each composed of four rows of townships taken vertically across the region. After calling for a December election of a Territorial Senate, the council enacted a series of laws regulating marriages and mortgages, and levying taxes. To simplify the matter, the laws of Colorado were adopted covering all other aspects of government. At their April 1887 meeting, the five council members present voted to send Dr. Orville G. Chase as a delegate to Congress to seek admission to the Union.

Unfortunately, the council's support was concentrated in the eastern portion of No Man's Land. Residents in the western half elected their own Territorial Council and a rival congressional delegate—J.E. Dale. The efforts of the two delegates hindered the movement for statehood and the one congressional bill calling for the recognition of the Territory of Cimarron failed. Other bills tried to attach No Man's Land to either Kansas or New Mexico. These also failed.

It was not until March 1889 that Congress placed No Man's Land under the jurisdiction of the Federal Court in Muskogee, 341 miles east of Beaver City. A year later, Congress created Oklahoma Territory and attached No Man's Land as County No. 7 to it, Beaver City being the county seat. With the convening of the First Territorial Legislature, County No. 7 was renamed Beaver County.

Beaver County governed the entire Panhandle until the Oklahoma Constitutional Convention of 1906.

At that time, the county's two delegates, Fred C. Tracy and T.C. James, recommended the division of the area into three counties—Beaver, Texas and Cimarron. Beaver City remained the seat of Beaver County, Guymon was named the seat of Texas County, and after a bitter county seat war among Boise City, Doby, Garlington and Hurley, Boise City was chosen as the seat for Cimarron County.

Beaver City remains one of the principal communities of the region. Its first residence dates from 1880 when Jim Lane built a two-room sod house and store, later incorporated into a six-room stucco structure that still stands. Another building still in use is the Beaver Presbyterian Church constructed in 1887. Both buildings are on The National Register of Historical Places.

In 1910, the Wichita Falls and Northwestern Railroad, which later became a part of the Missouri, Kansas and Texas Railroad (M-K-T), started building through the Panhandle. Bypassing Beaver the railroad established the community of Forgan in 1912 as the major shipping point in the area. Faced with losing a rail connection, Beaver-area citizens organized the Beaver, Meade and Englewood Railroad, which was built north from Beaver to Forgan, and later in the 1930s on to Keyes in Cimarron County. This railroad was so successful that it eventually was purchased by the M-K-T.

Another early-day Beaver County trading center was Slapout. Today a virtual ghost town, the community is said to have taken its name from a local merchant who often told customers: "I had it yesterday, but I'm slap out today." Gate, at the eastern edge of the Panhandle, takes its name from its description as the "gateway to the Neutral Strip," and was known as Gate City until 1894. Near Gate are silica mines.

Boise City, known as Cimarron until 1908, is the seat of Cimarron County, the only county in America that touches five states—Oklahoma, Kansas, Texas, Colorado and New Mexico. The community is closer to the capitals of Colorado, Kansas and New Mexico than to Oklahoma's capital. A quiet rural community until the arrival of the Atchison, Topeka and Santa Fe Railroad in 1925, Boise City became the major trading center of the region.

Guymon is one of the oldest settlements in No Man's Land. In the early 1880s, James K. Hitch, built a two-room sod house on nearby Coldwater Creek, and launched a ranching enterprise that today is one of the largest employers in the region. The original sod house was replaced in 1892 with a rock house boasting walls two feet thick. The cattle industry, pioneered by the Hitch family, is the mainstay of the area's economy and, in 1967, Swift and Company opened a packing plant in the community to handle the output of the numerous feed lots. Seaboard Corporation's $50 million plant in Guymon is capable of producing $800 million in pork products annually. Today Guymon and Texhoma are two of the nation's largest cattle markets.

Slightly northwest of Guymon is Optima, one of the oldest inhabited sites in Oklahoma. Near the community is the remains of a prehistoric settlement of Slab House People, who were among the earliest humans to inhabit the state. Optima is also the center of the Optima Wildlife Refuge.

Goodwell, southwest of Guymon, is the home of Panhandle Oklahoma State University. Although, the school became a four-year institution in 1925, it maintains its agricultural identity and operates a 2,000-acre experimental farm devoted to improving dry-land farming techniques. It also is the home of the No Man's Land Museum.

Hooker, named for cattleman Joseph Hooker, is another cattle and agriculture center of the Panhandle, located in Texas County. It also is the center of development of the prolific Guymon-Hugoton Gas Field, one of the nation's largest concentrations of natural gas and a major supplier of helium.

Located at the extreme northwestern corner of the Panhandle is Black Mesa—the dominant topographical feature of the region. It was formed by the eruption of a prehistoric volcano in what is now New Mexico. The resulting flow of black lava covered the area to a thickness of up to 70 feet. Volcanoes were so active in the prehistoric period that deposits of ash 40 feet thick can be found near Kenton. In the following eons, the erosion of the surrounding softer material left a rugged black-topped plateau standing 600 feet high. On top of the mesa is an 11-foot-tall obelisk giving an elevation of 4,972.97 feet above sea level—the highest elevation in Oklahoma.

As the most easily recognizable feature of the region, Black Mesa was a well-known gathering place for centuries, and the rugged terrain attracted outlaws. In 1863, General W.H. Penrose marked a road from Fort Lyon, Colorado, into the area in order to transport a cannon from the army post to Robber's Roost, a well-known outlaw hideout near Black Mesa. The route later became known as the Penrose Trail. Also nearby is the Devil's Tombstone, a 20-foot-high slab of brownish sandstone.

The beauty of the region is preserved as Black Mesa State Park, eight miles south of the rugged mesa. It includes the 200-acre Lake Carl Etling. Lava flows within the park contain prehistoric Native American pictographs and a dinosaur pit famous for its many bones of prehistoric creatures. Along the southern border of Cimarron County is the Rita Blanca Wildlife Management Area and South Cienequila Creek, the site of prehistoric Indian remains estimated to be 10,000 years old. Optima Reservoir, in Texas County, is another popular recreation site. The 6,000-acre lake has an 85-foot-high,

Above: Branding cattle on the Roberts Ranch in Cimarron County. Cattle, along with wheat and natural gas, are the basis for a rich economy that gives Cimarron County the state's highest per-capita income.

Right: The buckle on the wheat belt, the Oklahoma Panhandle is one of the richest wheat-producing areas in the world.

Above: *Huge quantities of hay are produced by Panhandle farmers for use by feedlots.*

Left: *Beaver, Oklahoma, the "Cow Chip Capital of the World," hosts an annual cow chip throwing contest. Because of the scarcity of timber, early-day settlers in No Man's Land used dried cow chips as a replacement fuel.*

16,875-foot-long earth dam that creates a lake with 31 miles of shoreline.

The entire Panhandle has an elevation of at least 2,000 feet above sea level and marks the beginning of a gradual slope downward that sees the topography of the state drop to 305 feet above sea level at the extreme southeast corner. Because every increase in elevation of 65 feet results in an average temperature drop of 1°, the Panhandle is one of the coldest areas of the state. The Panhandle has the highest average snowfall for the state, some 20 inches annually. It is also one of the driest areas of Oklahoma, with an average of 15.2 inches of rain falling during 45 days per year. Regnier in Cimarron County with 6.53 inches of rain has the lowest yearly rainfall every recorded in the state.

Unlike the rest of Oklahoma, surveyed from the Indian Meridian, the Panhandle land surveys were based on the Cimarron Meridian (the extreme western border of the state) and the Cimarron Base Line, at the southern border of the Oklahoma Panhandle.

Agriculture is the dominant industry in the Panhandle and irrigation is the principal source of water for its farmers. The region's major aquifer, the Ogallala Formation, provides adequate water for intensive farming operations. Its value to local farmers is estimated at more than $1 million. Today the Panhandle is the center of a thriving wheat-livestock-grain sorghum agribusiness that pours millions of dollars annually into the local economy. Most Panhandle farmers and ranchers utilize a combination of winter wheat and cattle to create a two-product economy. The wheat provides forage for the cattle during fall and winter (a diet supplemented by hay and processed feed) and in the spring the cattle are withdrawn from the wheat and marketed, providing one crop. Then the wheat is harvested for the second crop. Texas County is one of the state's leading meat-producing regions and numerous feed-lot operations dot the Panhandle. Not only does the meat cattle industry produce valuable income, but it provides a source for the Panhandle's meat packing industry. Guymon is one of the largest meat packing centers.

Texas County ranks first among the state's 77 counties in the production of meat cattle, fifth in oats and wheat, and is a leading producer of hay, with its farmers growing in excess of 75 million tons annually. In the production of wheat, both Texas and Beaver county farmers grow more than 6 million bushels every year, while Cimarron County produces between 3 million and 6 million bushels annually. Cimarron County also leads the state in barley production, and Texas, Cimarron and Beaver counties rank first, second and third, respectively, in the state in the production of grain sorghum.

The greatest natural resources of the Panhandle are its natural beauty, rich agricultural land, natural gas, and resourceful people. All of these combine to make the Panhandle one of the wealthiest area of the state. Cimarron and Beaver counties rank first and fifth in the state in per capita income. Cimarron County's 3,300 residents make an average of $24,606 per year. Most of this is represented in agricultural income. Cimarron County farmers and ranchers earn over $39 million of the county's $81.1 million in total income annually. While the Panhandle's short-grass carpet of level tablelands and rolling hills produce a bountiful crop of wild flowers and animal life that flood the region with color in the spring, grain elevators towering above all are the skyscrapers of the plains and the symbol of the wealth and bounty of this rich land.

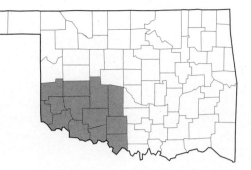

THE LURE OF THE WICHITAS
SOUTHWESTERN OKLAHOMA

Dominating southwestern Oklahoma is the Wichita Mountain Range—which includes the Wichita and Quartz mountains—that stretches from the Texas Panhandle across Harmon, Greer, Kiowa and Comanche counties. All that remains of the once mighty Wichitas are sunken mountain peaks, their sides having been buried by erosion over hundreds of millions of years. These weather-sculpted domes are covered with little vegetation and on average they stand between 650 and 700 feet high, with the highest, Mount Scott, rising to 2,464 feet.

The Wichitas are also the home of the Wichita Mountain Wildlife Refuge. Containing 59,099 acres northwest of Lawton, the refuge originally was set aside in 1901 as a forest reserve. To allow access to its scenic beauty, a winding drive is open though the refuge, which is filled with wildlife, including buffalo, elk, deer, longhorn cattle, wild turkeys and prairie dogs.

The Wichitas are one of the most extensive mineralized areas in the Southwest. Hematite and opals are found in Comanche County and at Government Quarry in Kiowa County. Copper once was mined at the Kiowa Copper Company's mine east of Roosevelt, and galena was produced from the Clark and Bennett mine in Comanche County. Pearls also are found along streams in Comanche, Jackson and Kiowa counties. It was the lure of gold, however, that first brought non-Indians into the Wichita range and gave the region its Southwestern heritage.

Southwestern Oklahoma was well-known to Spaniards. In 1541 Cristobel de Onate, a member of Francisco de Coronado's expedition, visited the region. Onate reported on a number of large, well-established Native American villages, including San Bernardo, which held as many as 4,000 Wichitas. Although the church looked upon the region as a rich source of converts, it was the quest for gold, not souls, that brought the Spanish to the Wichita Mountains.

Because they were the first mountains encountered by Spaniards moving north from Texas and east from New Mexico, the Wichitas were extensively prospected. As early as 1650, Spanish miners probed the

Employees of the Campbell gold mine. The horse-powered winch was used to raise the ore bucket from the bottom of the 75-foot-deep shaft on the north side of Mount Scott. The Wichitas were the scene of one of the last gold rushes to the American West between 1894 and 1904.

Above: Wild turkeys, such as this gobbler, have also been reintroduced into southwestern Oklahoma.
Right: A part of the buffalo herd in the Wichita Mountains National Wildlife Refuge. In 1905 President Theodore Roosevelt set aside the area as a wildlife preserve and two years later 15 buffalo were transferred from the New York Zoological Park to help reestablish the shaggy beasts in a region where millions once roamed.
Top: Scenic Treasure Lake deep within the Wichita Mountains National Wildlife Refuge.

WARREN NEWELL

Moonrise over the rugged Wichita Mountains.

Mount Scott in the Wichitas has always attracted tourists. This panorama was taken in 1900.

Wichitas searching for gold. According to legend, one of the first was a Father Gilbert, who led a party of one hundred men into the Wichitas, in 1657. Searching for gold or silver, they reportedly sunk a 100-foot deep shaft near Mount Scott. More than a century later, in 1765, a Frenchman named Brevel visited the region and reported that Spaniards were working mines in the mountains. Today several primitive mine shafts can be seen in the region. South of Meers on the northern bank of Medicine Creek are the ruins of a Spanish arrastra, a crude mill used to separate gold ore from host rock.

The first Americans to penetrate the Wichitas were probably Simon N. Cockrell and William Bean in 1833. They reported that there were Mexican miners at work near Devil's Canyon. In his book *Commerce of the Prairies,* published in 1844, Josiah Gregg described silver ore taken from old Spanish mines in the Wichitas, and in 1850, William Kyle, a surveyor from Vernon, Texas, reported a Mexican silver mine near Navajoe Mountain. Native Americans tales abound with Spanish and Mexican miners in the Wichitas, and vicious battles as the Indians tried to drive the foreigners from their land. Strange carvings found on rocks and trees and Indian petroglyphs in the region reportedly tell the secrets of mines and hidden caches of abandoned treasure.

One of the most famous of the hidden mines of the Wichitas is the lost cave with the iron door. Tradition maintains that the cave is filled with millions of dollars in gold that Spanish miners were forced to abandon when they fled from Indian raiders. During the 1850s a Mexican appeared in the Wichitas with a secret map and searched the area extensively. The hunt was cut short by an Indian uprising and the Mexican and his map disappeared. Several other adventurers have claimed to have seen the huge iron door barring entrance to the cave, but so far no one has recovered the treasure.

Many of the signs and relics of early mining activity were found near Devil's Canyon, north of the Red River opposite Suttles Mountain, and between Flattop and Soldier's Spring mountains. Here, the remains of mines, crucibles, and human skeleton were found in the late nineteenth century, and possibly the ruins of a non-Indian settlement and a Spanish mission.

Another of the Wichitas' famous lost treasures resulted from the Battle of Cutthroat Gap in Comanche County. Early in 1833, a war party of Kiowas, on the Santa Fe Trail, attacked a trading caravan carrying $10,000 in silver coins. After the fight, the Kiowas gathered up the money and returned to their camp on Otter Creek in Cutthroat Gap. Later, Osage warriors attacked the Kiowa village while most of the men were away hunting. Decapitating their victims, the Osages put their victims' heads in brass buckets and left them on the battle site. When the Kiowas returned they buried those killed, along with their share of the silver. The treasure has never been uncovered.

Later, the Wichitas became well-known hideouts for such outlaws as Jesse and Frank James, Cole Younger, Bud Dalton and others. Legends of caches of ill-gotten booty hidden in the Wichitas abound. In 1948, at the base of Tarbone Mountain, a buried kettle was unearthed that supposedly contained the key to the James boys treasure, but no gold was found.

Following the Mexican War, hostile Indians and the strengthening American claim to the Southwest caused the Spanish and Mexican mines to be abandoned prior to the American Civil War. Following the Reconstruction Treaties with the Five Tribes, the area was set aside as a home for the Plains tribes; in 1867, the Comanche, Kiowa and Apache Reservation that included the Wichitas was created. Until the opening of the region to homesteaders in 1901 prospecting was limited.

Some prospectors, however, still braved sometimes hostile Indians and government restrictions. One was A.J. Meers, who settled in Greer County in 1885 and sought for two decades to unravel some of the Wichitas' secrets. Another, James Hale, in 1889 located the Golden Run Copper Mine. The ruins of Hale's mine still can be seen northeast of Oreana, where the Wichita Mountains Wildlife Refugee Scenic Highway passes through Buffalo Gap.

The discovery of silver in Devil's Canyon by a party of Colorado miners in 1892 reignited the mining frenzy. Their mine, the Oriental, in what became the Eureka Gold Mining District, was located near Quartz Mountain in Greer County. Another nearby mine, the Silver Ledge, gave rise to the town of Silverton, thirteen miles east of Mangum. Reportedly its ore assayed as high as $140 per ton in gold and silver.

The belief that the Wichitas contained veins of gold was to cause one of the last mineral rushes in the United States. The stampede started in August 1901 and as many as 20,000 miners flocked to the region. Nine gold mining districts eventually were established before the boom ended in 1904.

The Cache Gold Mining District, located in the Quanah Range in Comanche County north of the town of Cache, reported mines producing as much as $36 of gold per ton of ore. The remains of a 25-ton ore smelter built by John Pearson on the slope of Mount Sherman northeast of Cache still can be seen. Craterville, located about three miles northeast of Cache boasted a population of three hundred during the rush. The Florence Mine assayed 61 percent zinc, 8 percent lead, and $58 per ton of gold, but mines such as the Grubstank, Peacock, Accident and Galena soon proved unproductive and were abandoned.

Cache's Craterville Park, a large natural amphitheatre, hosted the first All-Indian Fair and Exposition, in 1924. Eagle Park, north of Cache, offers both recreational facilities and a re-creation of an early-day pioneer "picket house." Close by is Comanche Chief Quanah Parker's home. The chief was the son of Cynthia Ann Parker, who had been captured by the Comanches at the age of nine. Quanah Parker, when told by a government official to give up all of his wives but one, said, "You tell me which one I keep!" The matter was pursued no further.

The Cooperton Gold Mining District was centered around the town of Cooperton. Not an extensively mined area, the Oasis and other mines were abandoned by 1904. To the south, in Comanche County, the Meers Gold Mining District was on the east slope of the Wichitas around the town of Meers. Founded by A.J. Meers, the town lay at the northern base of Mount Sheridan. Between 1901 and 1904 it was the most extensive of the state's gold mining districts and claimed such mines as the Lost Lead, the Teddy, the Ethel, the Red Cedar, the Green Lead, and the Snake. Some of the discoveries initially assayed at $105 per ton.

The Mountain Park Gold Mining District's most promising site was located at Poverty Gulch, northwest of Medicine Park. Others prospects were found on Rattlesnake Mountain. Much of the activity in the Oreana Gold Mining District was centered around Sugar Tit Mountain, east of Oreana. The Lone Star Mining Company and the Oreana Mining and Milling Company were its major developers. Some assays were reported averaging more than $100 of gold per ton.

The Roosevelt Gold Mining District, between Roosevelt and Cold Springs, was one of the most thoroughly exploited gold-mining districts of Kiowa County. Miners began digging as early as 1894 and development continued for two decades. Southwest of the post office at Cold Springs was the Culberson Mining Company's No. 1 Shaft, which was sunk to a depth of eighty feet. Other mines included the Alpha, the Copper King and the Green Horn.

In southern Kiowa County the Snyder Gold Mining District's Meek, Anderson and Laughlin Mine was the deepest gold mine in the Wichitas. It was abandoned at 220 feet. Other mines included the Big Stone, Little Maud, Lost Mexican and many other shallow diggings. Nearby the Wildman Gold Mining District was named for the town of Wildman, founded by Frank Wildman. The town's main street was just south of Nest Egg Mountain. Lightning Gulch, near Roosevelt, claimed assays as high as $23 of gold per ton. Within the town of Wildman, miners sunk the Gold Coin Mine. Other mines included the Lone Jack, Post Oak, Gold Hill, Twin Rose, Good Luck, and the Peach Blossom. Most were abandoned by 1904. The massive remains of the Gold Bell Mining and Milling Company can be seen nine miles west of Snyder.

Below: A gnarled juniper on Elk Mountain in the Charons Garden Wilderness in the Wichita Mountains National Wildlife Refuge.

Facing page: Dawn at Altus Lake in Quartz Mountain State Park in southwestern Oklahoma.

TOM TILL

During the gold rush more than 2,500 mine shafts were sunk in the Wichitas. Hundreds of small furnaces for smelting the ore were built and hundreds of thousands of dollars were invested in the search for riches before the boom busted. Although by 1904 most of the miners had abandoned the area, leaving their mines and equipment to decay, as late as 1917 prospectors were dredging placer gold from creeks feeding the North Fork of the Red River and Deep Red Creek in Kiowa and Tillman counties.

Just as the gold rush ended another began. This time it was "black gold"—oil—that brought tens of thousands of wildcatters pouring into southwestern Oklahoma. Oil was not new to the area. For centuries Native Americans used the region's oil and natural gas seeps in their ceremonies and as medicine. Boyd Springs, on Oil Creek, northeast of Ardmore was a favorite campground. A tube or gun barrel was often forced into the ground to tap the escaping natural gas. As the gas spewed out of the end of the barrel, it was set afire to provide illumination.

Wheeler Spring, one of the largest natural oil springs in the United States, is located north of Oil City in what became the Sho-Vel-Tum Oil Field. It, and other seeps, became the center of a thriving "medicine spring" business. Hotels were constructed to cater to those arriving to "take the cure" at such places as Thomas Boyd's and Overton Love's Oil Springs Resort Hotel near Hickory Creek southeast of Ardmore.

In 1872, Robert M. Darden formed the Chickasaw Oil Company to develop the area's oil deposits, but was thwarted by federal officials who refused to allow Indians to lease their land. In 1888, a man named Palmer drilled one of the first wells in Oklahoma, and struck oil at 400 feet, in what later became the prolific Healdton Field. The well was on restricted Indian land and he, like Darden, was unable to secure a lease. With the allotment of tribal lands, the situation changed; in 1905 the Coline Oil Company uncovered the Wheeler Oil Field. Oil City became a thriving oil boom town, as pioneer oilmen such as Charles F. Colcord rushed to the site. It was the rediscovery of the Healdton Field, however, that touched off the mad scramble for riches.

After hearing stories of Palmer's earlier well, Roy M. Johnson, A.T. McGhee and Edward Galt located his abandoned well in 1911. When they removed the bucket that covered the well-head, oil flowed out. Joining with Samuel A. Apple and Wirt Franklin, they brought in the field's first producer in July 1913. Healdton's output was so great—it was the twenty-fourth largest field located in the nation prior to 1950 and during its heyday produced almost 211 million barrels of crude—that it overwhelmed local facilities and hundreds of thousands of barrels of crude were stored awaiting shipment. This tremendous glut resulted in the field's August Hell in 1914. The inferno was touched off on August 12 when a thunderstorm swept the area and lightning ignited several fires that spread to the open-pit oil storage sites and 55,000-barrel storage tanks. The fire could be seen for miles, and an estimated 400,000 barrels of oil burned before the fire was brought under control sixteen days later.

Healdton's twin discovery, the Hewitt Oil Field, was opened in June 1919, when The Texas Company completed the A.E. Denney No. 1 southeast of Dillard. When combined with the West Hewitt Oil Field, the two pools were the seventieth largest discovery made in the nation in the first half of the twentieth

century, having a combined output of more than 109 million barrels.

Wirt was the wildest boom town of the Healdton Field. It was located along a section line road, later named Texas Road, just west of Healdton. Called Ragtown because of the large number of tents used as dwellings, Wirt acquired a reputation for "wild women and whiskey," and housed a multitude of brothels, gambling dens, saloons and dance halls catering to oil-field workers. Today the remains of the Pure Oil Company Gas Booster Station can be seen south of Texas Road.

The Oil Field Railroad, or Ringling Railroad, was built in 1917 by John Ringling, of circus fame, and Jake Hammon as a spur line from Cobalt Junction, just west of Jointer City, through the center of the Healdton Field to the town of Healdton to haul supplies to the surrounding wells. Ringling in Carter County was named for the circus owner.

Ardmore, seat of Carter County and the center of the Healdton-Hewitt boom, was an established commercial center prior to the nearby discovery of oil and became the supply point for the nearby fields. It was the home of such oilmen as Charles B. Goddard, Wirt Franklin, Lloyd Noble, Ward S. Merrick, Leon Daube, Walter Neustadt and Max Westheimer. Robert A. Hefner, Sr. was a prominent independent oilman who served as the mayor of Ardmore and developer the Hefner Form, which separated oil and gas minerals from fee simple title to property. Later moving to

Southwestern Oklahoma always offered a plentiful supply of wildlife. These huge catfish were caught in the Washita River east of Chickasha in the early 1900s.

was west of the Cross Timbers, very few non-Indian settlers penetrated the area. The first official American contact with the Native American inhabitants of southwestern Oklahoma came with the Dragoon Expedition of 1834. Commanded by Brigadier General Henry Leavenworth and Colonel Henry Dodge, five hundred troopers of the First Dragoon Regiment left Fort Gibson in June 1834, to establish relations with the Kiowa, Comanches and other Plains Indians. Dressed in close-fitting wool uniforms, the Dragoons suffered from the heat of summer and almost half of the command was ill by the time the expedition reached Camp Washita on the border of southwestern Oklahoma. Leavenworth, who had been injured, was unable to continue and remained behind with half the troopers, while Dodge and the rest pressed on. Eventually the Dragoons arrived at the Wichita village on the North Fork of the Red River in Kiowa County, where Dodge convinced the Indians to send delegates to Fort Gibson for a council.

Relations between Indians and non-Indians remained tense for almost half a century, and, as Americans came into increasing contact with the Native Americans, there were several sharp skirmishes. One of the most notable, the Battle of the Wichita Village, took place in October 1858, along the banks of Rush Creek in Grady County. Seventy Comanches were killed in the fighting. Today Rush Springs is better known as a center of watermelon production.

To keep watch over the potentially hostile Indians, Camp Radziminsky was established in Kiowa County in September 1858. No permanent buildings were built and the men were sheltered in huts. The camp was abandoned in December 1859, but with the outbreak of the Civil War it was reoccupied by Texas Rangers and other Confederate units.

In 1855, the federal government leased all the land west of the 98th meridian from the Choctaw and Chickasaw. Known as the Leased District, it became the home of the Wichita, Tawakoni, Waco, Anadarko, Caddo, Hainai, Kichai and affiliated tribes, which were administered by the Wichita Agency, the first Indian agency in western Oklahoma. At the outbreak of the Civil War, the Wichita Agency was the location of Confederate Albert Pike's negotiations with the eleven tribes served by the agency that allied themselves with the South. In 1862, a force of pro-Northern Indians

Oklahoma City, he donated the family home to the Oklahoma Heritage Association. His son Robert A. Hefner, Jr., continued to operate his family's oil operations, and his grandson, Robert A. Hefner III, pioneered drilling in the Deep Anadarko Basin in southwestern Oklahoma and the resulting energy boom of the 1970s and 1980s. At one time, Ardmore boasted that it was the home of more millionaires per capita than any other community in America.

On September 27, 1915, the Ardmore Casinghead Gasoline Explosion reduced the community's business district to rubble, killed forty-three people and injured 450 others. The blast was triggered by a leaking railroad tank-car filled with volatile cashinghead gasoline. The hot sun turned the casinghead gasoline into a vapor that exploded. The blast led to a nationwide demand for greater regulation of the casinghead gasoline industry.

Northwest of the Healdton discovery is Duncan. Founded as a depot on the Chicago, Rock Island and Pacific Railroad in 1892, Duncan boomed during the 1920s as the headquarters of Halliburton Services and as the center for the development of the nearby Sho-Vel-Tum oil field.

Prior to statehood, however, southwestern Oklahoma was the domain of Native Americans. Because it destroyed the agency and massacred the pro-Southern Tonkawas camped nearby.

Fort Cobb was established in 1859 by Colonel William H. Emory to protect the nearby Wichita Agency It was abandoned by federal troops in May 1861 and Southern officials enlisted several Comanches into Confederate service as guards for the agency until it was abandoned in 1862. Reoccupied after the Civil War, Fort Cobb was abandoned finally in 1869.

Camp Napoleon, at Verden in Grady County, was the site of the May 1865 meeting between representatives of the pro-Southern Cherokee, Choctaw, Creek, Seminole, Chickasaw, Caddo, Osage and Comanche Indians and leaders of the Plains Kiowa, Arapaho, Cheyenne, Lipan, Caddo, Comanche and Anadarko. More than five thousand Indians attended the meeting, which produced a peace compact among the tribes at the close of the Civil War.

Following the Civil War, southwestern Oklahoma was stripped from the Chickasaws and the federal government began a policy of concentrating Plains Indians in the region. As a result a number of Indian reservations were created, including the Comanche, Kiowa and Apache Reservation. It occupied the region east of the North Fork of the Red River, west of the 98th meridian, south of the Washita River and north of the Cheyenne-Arapaho Reservation. To keep watch on the tribes, Camp Robinson, east of Camp Radziminsky in Kiowa County, was established in 1871. The most famous of these frontier posts was Fort Sill, north of Lawton, the county seat of Comanche County and the third-largest metropolitan area in Oklahoma. Established in January 1869 along Cache Creek at the edge of the Wichita Mountains, Fort Sill was a major staging area for Indian campaigns throughout Oklahoma and Texas.

Beginning in 1902, the United States Army transformed Fort Sill into its main artillery training center. The Fort Sill Museum is filled with exhibits illustrating the history of Fort Sill, and the nearby Cannon Walk is lined with artillery pieces captured during the nation's wars.

In the modern era the military has continued to play a major role in the economic development of southwestern Oklahoma. Altus Air Force Base, west of Altus in Jackson County, was established as Altus Army Air Corps Field in 1942 and served as an advanced flight training facility throughout World War II. The base was closed following the war, but was reopened in 1953 as Altus AFB. In 1968, Altus AFB became a part of the Military Airlift Command and a training center for the giant C-5 and C-141 transport aircraft.

In 1956 Altus became the first community in Oklahoma to be named an "All American City." It is the center of a vast agricultural area watered by the huge Luger-Altus Irrigation system. Just north of Altus is Navajoe Mountain. At the base of the mountain is the town of Navajoe, the home of *Buckskin Joe's Emigrant Guide,* published in 1887, and at the time accepted as one of the best guides for travelers crossing the American West.

Next to the now-closed Clinton-Sherman AFB is the town of Clinton. Nearby was the Cheyenne and Arapaho Cattle Ranch, which leased more than a million acres for grazing in the 1890s. Southwest of Clinton is Colony, the home of the Dutch Reformed Church's Indian agricultural colony operated by John Segar.

Other missions were the Mennonite Brethren Home at Post Oak in Comanche County and St. Patrick's Mission School in Anadarko. Anadarko is a major center for the Bureau of Indian Affairs and is the home of the world-famous American Indian Exposition. Nearby on the Washita River is the Riverside Indian Boarding School.

The Native American claim to southwestern Oklahoma was challenged in the post-Civil War era by cattlemen. Cattle drives from Texas to northern markets had been interrupted by the fighting, but now the beef-starved North offered a ready market. Joseph G. McCoy, after building offices and shipping yards at Abiline, Kansas, circulated handbills throughout the Southwest asking for cattlemen to bring the herds north. The trail that McCoy used had been pioneered by federal troops, commanded by Colonel William H. Emory, that had marched north to Kansas at the outbreak of the Civil War. Emory was guided by the Delaware scouts Black Beaver and Possum. In 1865, Jesse Chisholm followed Emory's trail south from Kansas to trade with the Plains Indians, and cattlemen quickly adopted the route, which became known as the Chisholm Trail, as the major route to the Kansas railheads.

Just to the north of Waurika is Addington and the nearby 18,000-acre Price Ranch, settled in 1886 by H.J. Price, who constructed a large white colonial-style ranch house. A spring on the ranch became a familiar stopping place on the Chisholm Trail. Every time a cattle drive stopped at the spring, cowboys would pile rocks on a nearby hill. Now called Monument Hill, the pile of stones remains.

In 1876 a new cattle trail was opened—the Great Western. It struck the Red River at Doan's Store and followed the old buffalo migration route northward. The salt springs south of Erick were a well-known stopping place. Later the deposits were developed into a major supplier of commercial salt.

As the line of settlement moved westward and grass in Texas became scarce, the importance of southwestern Oklahoma's rich pasture land grew. Old Greer County quickly attracted the attention of Texas cattlemen. Prior to 1896, the area that included all of Jack-

son, Greer, Harmon and southern Beckham counties was a part of Texas. Beginning in 1881, Texas ranchers pastured cattle permanently in the region. Mangum, the county seat of Greer County, Texas, remained under the control of Texas until 1896, when the United States Supreme Court ruled the that the Prairie Dog Fork of the Red River was the main channel of the stream and that the area belonged to Oklahoma Territory. In 1897 the Greer County Homestead Act was passed by Congress, opening the area to settlement. At statehood, Old Greer County was broken into three separate counties—Jackson, Greer and a portion of Beckham.

Greer County land, however, was not sufficient to supply the needs of Texas cattlemen, and they moved onto the Comanche-Kiowa-Apache Reservation. The cattlemen ignored the orders of federal officials to remove their herds, and ranching became firmly established. When the Comanche-Kiowa-Apache Reservation was opened to settlers in 1891, 480,000 acres were reserved for use as a common grazing area by the cattlemen. Of this, 401,000 acres were set aside in one contiguous area. Called the Big Pasture, this region composed western Cotton County, southeastern Tillman County and a small portion of southern Comanche County. It was not until 1901 that the cattlemen were removed and the Big Pasture was opened to homesteaders by sealed bids.

By the mid-1880s most land suitable for farming in the American West had been claimed—land-hungry

settlers began to look toward Indian Territory. In 1889 Congress responded by opening the Unassigned Lands for settlement by a land run. This was followed by six other runs, including one on April 19, 1892 that opened the 3.5 million acres of the Cheyenne-Arapaho Reservation. The opening of the Cheyenne-Arapaho Reservation added C, D, E, F, G, and H counties to Oklahoma Territory. These were renamed Blaine, Dewey, Day, Roger Mills, Custer and Washita respectively, with Washita and the southern portion of Roger Mills being in southwestern Oklahoma.

Because of the confusion generated by the runs, the Comanche, Kiowa and Apache Reservation and the Wichita and Caddo Reservation were opened by lottery in 1901. This area was organized as Comanche, Kiowa and part of Caddo counties. In 1907, portions of Kiowa and Comanche counties were used to form Jackson County, while in 1910, Cotton County was created from southern Comanche County.

The early homesteaders in southwestern Oklahoma quickly developed a thriving agricultural economy. Many of them were Mennonite immigrants from Germany and Russia who brought with them the ability to adjust to the hot, dry climate. Bessie and Corn were

Above: Corn and Bessie in Washita County both retain their German heritage first brought to the region by Mennonite settlers in the nineteenth century.
Top: The "skyscrapers of the Plains"—a grain elevator rises from the fertile ground of southwestern Oklahoma. In the foreground is a cotton field. Altus, in Jackson County, is the center of a rich cotton-producing area.

Facing page: An aged Eastern red cedar clinging to the wind-swept summit of Mount Scott.

centers of their settlements. Corn originally was spelled Korn, but during the patriotic zeal of World War I, its spelling was anglicized.

The drastic wet and dry cycles, however, proved difficult obstacles. Dust storms, hail storms, high winds, spring deluges and numerous other hazards were faced. Most farmers turned to cash crops, and cotton became "king." Altus, Ardmore and Mangum became major cotton centers. Chickasha also developed a major cotton market and, as the center of a large cottonseed oil industry, became the home of the Chickasha Cotton Oil Company that operated throughout the Southwest. In 1908, the Oklahoma College for Women, present-day University of Arts and Science of Oklahoma, was established in the community.

Cotton still dominates southwestern Oklahoma, with Jackson, Tillman, Harmon, Washita and Kiowa counties ranking first, second, third, fourth and fifth in production. Hollis in Harmon County is the location of a huge cotton-oil mill, which processes animal feed for export worldwide. Frederick, the seat of Tillman County, is another major cotton producing center. It was also the site of Theodore Roosevelt's famous wolf hunt in 1905.

As extensive cultivation destroyed much of the native grass cover, erosion and flooding became serious problems. To correct this, several conservation and reclamation projects were launched. The Washita River was America's first river system to be treated with watershed flood-control lakes. The nation's first upstream flood-control dam was completed on Cloud Creek in 1948.

During the later decades of the twentieth century the region's farmers diversified and peanuts became a major crop. Farms around Carnegie, Binger, Eakly and Hinton produce more than $2 million worth of peanuts annually. Garvin and Grady counties are major suppliers of broomcorn. In the past, the international price of broomcorn was based on the harvest-time price in Lindsay. Waurika is known as the "Parakeet Capital of the World" and each year local dealers handle in excess of 850,000 parakeets.

Hinton is famous for nearby scenic canyons—including Red Rock Canyon State Park, one of the most colorful sheer-walled canyons in the state. A favorite camping site for emigrants on the California Trail, numerous carvings by the 49ers can be seen on the red sandstone ledges. Nearby Rock Mary was named in honor of Mary Conway by two officers accompanying Captain Randolph B. Marcy when he surveyed the California Road in 1849. The stone outcrop became a major milestone on the long overland trek.

Southwestern Oklahoma contains a diversity of geography and history. Claimed by Plains Indians, explored by conquistadors and occupied by cattlemen, it is more Southwestern in flavor than other parts of the state. This distinct blending of cowboy and Indians marks the beginning of the Wild West and gives the region a unique rich and colorful Western heritage.

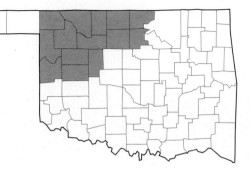

SHORT GRASS COUNTRY
NORTHWESTERN OKLAHOMA

The Short Grass country of northwestern Oklahoma is characterized by gently sloping prairie covered with native grasses and cut with steep-walled canyons and eroded peaks, ridges and mesas. A natural pasture land, the region was buffalo country. So many of the beasts grazed the rich prairie that early explorers reported herds twenty-five miles wide and fifty miles long that took five days to pass a given point and contained an estimated 12 million animals.

Among the region's prominent features are the Antelope Hills, six irregular peaks in a horseshoe bend in the Canadian River that mark the 100th meridian, once the western border of the United States and the Glass (or Gloss) Mountains, so named because of their selenite crystals that reflect different colors of light. They are a part of the Gypsum Hills that stretch 100 miles along the North Fork of the Canadian River. The largest of the Glass Mountains is Cathedral Mountain, a 300-foot-high gypsum butte. Roman Nose State Park, centered around the Spring of Everlasting Water, once a favorite campsite of Native Americans, is in the heart of the Gypsum Hills. Located in Cedar Canyon, south of Freedom, Alabaster Cavern is one of the world's largest gypsum caves. Some 200 million years old, it is lined with white stone and pink alabaster and sparkling selenite crystals. Cedar Canyon's natural bridge stands 150 feet above the canyon floor.

The Grand Saline, or Great Salt Plains, in Alfalfa County, is a vast expanse of white salt, which was highly prized by Native Americans and early homesteaders. In 1941 the Great Salt Plains Reservoir was constructed. Along its banks is the 33,000-acre Salt Plains National Wildlife Refuge. The three-mile-wide, twelve-mile-long Little Salt Plain, or Rock Saline, is located along the Cimarron River in Harper and Woods counties.

Scattered among the rich grazing lands of the Short Grass country are a number of natural springs—Boiling Springs, near Woodward—that gush cool, clear water. The region is drained by the Cimarron, North Fork of the Canadian, the Salt Fork of the

Arkansas, Canadian and Wichita rivers. Along the riverbanks is the Western Sand Dune Belt. In some places, such as Little Sahara State Recreation Area in Woods County, the prevailing southwestern winds have formed the sand into towering dunes.

It was the presence of the huge herds of buffalo that attracted the buffalo Indians to northwestern Oklahoma. Their entire culture evolved around the buffalo and the horse. Northwestern Oklahoma was in the center of their ancient hunting grounds.

In the post-Civil War era, the buffalo Indians and non-Indians clashed over the control of the Short Grass country. The fighting started in the summer of 1867 and lasted until that fall when the Treaties of Medicine Lodge were signed. Under the provisions of these agreements, the Cheyenne-Arapaho were granted a reservation in Dewey, Blaine, Custer, Roger Mills, northern Beckham and southern Ellis counties.

Hostilities resumed during the spring of 1868, and to force the Cheyenne and Arapaho back onto the reservation, the federal government mounted a massive military operation. Camp Supply, in present-day Woodward County, was established in November by Brevet Brigadier General George Armstrong Custer as his supply base. Expanded and renamed Fort Supply in 1889, it was abandoned in 1893. The major engagement of the 1868 Plains Indian war was the Battle of the Washita, in present-day Roger Mills County, in November 1868; Custer attacked Black Kettle's band of Cheyenne. Custer suffered 34 casualties, while 153 Indians were killed, their village burned and their horses captured. Demoralized, the Cheyenne and Arapaho returned to their reservation.

The Plains Indians were not alone in hunting in northwestern Oklahoma. The Cherokee had made periodic hunting trips into the region for years, and in the early nineteenth century they were granted a route—the Cherokee Outlet—to the buffalo-hunting grounds west to the 100th meridian. Although the area had been reserved for the Indians, in the 1870s non-Indians entered the area in search of buffalo. The beasts' hides and tongues were in great demand, selling for between $1 and $4. A capable hunter could easily kill fifty buffalo a day. The hides and tongues were taken and the meat left to rot. The slaughter was huge and within two decades the buffalo were exterminated.

The destruction of the buffalo touched off the Red River War of 1874. Another minor outbreak took place in 1878, when the Northern Cheyenne, who had been removed to Indian Territory following their participation in the Sioux War of 1876-1877, attempted to return to their homeland. Caught, they were returned to the Cheyenne-Arapaho Reservation until 1883.

Cantonment, just east of Canton Lake in Blaine County, was established in March 1879, to prevent any future attempt by the Northern Cheyenne to leave their reservation. Three stone buildings were built—a commissary, a hospital and officers quarters; the troops lived in sod huts. Cantonment was abandoned in June 1882, and the buildings transferred to a Mennonite Indian school. In 1885, the post was reoccupied because of trouble between the Cheyenne and Arapaho and nearby ranchers.

By the end of the Indian wars of the 1870s the buffalo had been destroyed, leaving a vast expanse of rich grazing land. Into the vacuum came the cattlemen. Cattlemen had been traveling through the region for more than a decade over the Chisholm and Great Western trails. Caddo Springs, Buffalo Springs and Sewell's Stockade were well-known landmarks. One of the area's oldest settlements, Sewell's Stockade, south of Medford, was established in 1866 as an Indian trading post on the Black Dog Trail. In 1879, the settlement's post office was named Pond, because of the large pond next to the stockade, and the community became known as Pond Creek. Later Pond Creek Station was moved three miles to the south.

By 1889, the new Pond Creek was the southern terminal of the Chicago, Rock Island and Pacific Railroad. The local depot was called Round Pond. To accommodate 89ers wanting to make the Run of '89, the railroad commissioned D.R. Green to gather wagons at new Pond Creek to carry them to the Unassigned Lands. Green met the train with a collection of stagecoaches, wagons, hacks, buggies and buckboards onto which the hopeful homesteaders were piled for the trip south. In 1893, Pond Creek was named the seat of Grant County.

As grazing range became scarce in Texas, ranchers negotiated leases with the tribes of northwestern Oklahoma. Early in 1883, seven ranchers—Lewis M. Briggs, Edward Fenlon, William E. Malaley, Hampton B. Denman, Albert G. Evans, Robert D. Hunter and Jesse Morrison—leased 3,117,880 acres for ten years at a cost of 2¢ per acre from the Cheyenne-Arapaho. More than 300,000 head of cattle grazed on the reservation until 1885 when the leases were canceled by President Grover Cleveland. Cattlemen, however, con-

Black Kettle National Grasslands in Rogers Mills County contains almost 3,000 lakes amid its 30,826-acres of preserve. The rolling high plains once was the home of the Cheyenne and Arapaho who hunted the vast herds of buffalo grazing on the rich grassland.

from the tribes living west of the Five Tribes. That same year the Cherokee (or Jerome) Commission was appointed to negotiate with the Cherokees for the secession of the Cherokee Outlet; however, it quickly expanded its jurisdiction to all tribes in Indian Territory.

In the fall of 1890 the Cheyenne-Arapaho agreed to allotment and the sale of the surplus lands for $1.5 million. Congress approved the agreement in March 1891, and within a year, 3,329 allotments of 160 acres each—totaling 230,000 acres—had been made. Another 32,000 acres were withheld by the government for agency grounds and military posts. The remaining 3.5 million acres were available for homesteading.

The Cheyenne-Arapaho had taken most of the land along the North Fork of the Canadian and Canadian rivers. Much of the remainder was undeveloped, rough, hilly, arid, and outside of railroad service. As a result, only about 25,000 people participated in the Cheyenne-Arapaho Run, and most of them staked claims in the eastern half of the reservation.

Blaine County's southern border originally was the North Fork of the Canadian River; however, after the opening of the Wichita-Caddo Reservation in 1901, the extreme northwestern portion of that reservation was added to Blaine County. Settled on the day of the opening, Watonga was the home of Oklahoma Territorial Governor Thomas B. Ferguson, the editor of the *Watonga Republican*. The region developed a major dairy industry and the Blaine Dairy Products plant is one of only three cheese processing facilities in the state.

A large number of Mennonites homesteaded near Geary. East of Geary is Coyote Hill, a prominent red-sandstone butte that was a meeting place for the Cheyenne and Arapaho during the Ghost Dance movement

tinued to use the reservation without legal authority until 1891 when the Cheyenne-Arapaho were granted individual allotments and the surplus land was opened to homesteaders.

In 1887, the Dawes Act had allowed the president to allot land in severalty to any tribe he considered sufficiently "advanced." In 1889, the Springer Amendment authorized the president to negotiate for the purchase of all surplus land not needed for allotments of 1890. An iron bedstead, springs, mattress and blankets were placed on top of Coyote Hill by the Indians to await use by the messiah the Ghost Dancers had promised.

North of Watonga is Southard, where the United States Gypsum Company opened a quarry in 1905, and Bickford, another company town that served the Roman Nose Gypsum Company's mill. Okeene in far northern Blaine County is best known for its annual rattlesnake round-up and banquet. Carry Nation, the famous prohibitionist, once lived in a two-story log cabin west of Seiling.

Arapaho is the seat of Custer County and for more than a decade dominated the economy of the region. In 1903, however, the Chicago, Rock Island and Pacific Railroad bypassed Arapaho in favor of Clinton. Clinton, organized in 1903 with the arrival of the railroad, was originally called Washita Junction. It was the junction of three railroads—the Chicago, Rock Island and Pacific; the St. Louis and San Francisco; and the Clinton, Oklahoma and Western. Established in 1893, the nearby Cheyenne and Arapaho Ranch grazed more than 1 million acres and was one of the largest ranches in Oklahoma.

Weatherford, in eastern Custer County, is the home of Southwestern Oklahoma State University. The community was established in 1898 as a rough railroad town that boasted fourteen saloons within two months of its founding. The productive farmland was settled by colonies of Amish, Old Mennonites, Dunkards and River Brethren. Nearby the River Brethren operated the Jabbok Bible School and Orphanage until 1955.

The two other counties created from the Cheyenne-Arapaho Reservation—Day and Roger Mills—had several boundary adjustments. The officials who originally drew the county's boundaries relied on township and range lines and ignored the region's only natural boundary—the Canadian River. Half of Day County was north of the river and the other half to the south. There were few bridges during this early period and frequent floods effectively divided the county into two parts. At statehood, Day County was divided. The area south of the Canadian River formed Roger Mills County and the northern part of Beckham County. North of the river was added to the western half of Woodward County to form Ellis County.

Arnett, Ellis County's seat, is a major broomcorn and dairy producing area. West of Arnett, the Burnett Gristmill, built by W.F. Burnett in 1900, remained operational until 1925. Nearby is the site of the Battle of Antelope Hills, which took place in 1858 between Texas Rangers and a band of Comanches. Iron Jacket, the Comanche Chief who acquired his name by wearing a jacket of Spanish mail, was killed in the fight. Nearby Shattuck was settled in by German immigrants from Russia.

Cheyenne was named the seat of Roger Mills County. The home of the Black Kettle Museum, Cheyenne is surrounded by the Black Kettle National Grasslands. In the mid-1950s, the Sand Stone Creek system near Cheyenne was the first completed watershed flood-control system in the nation.

The largest of the Indian lease arrangements in Indian Territory took place in the Cherokee Outlet. Beginning in 1880, a series of meetings were held in Caldwell, Kansas, to discuss common problems among these cattlemen. As a offshoot, in 1883, the ranchers formed the Cherokee Strip Live Stock Association— one of the largest (if not the largest) organizations in the world dedicated to the cattle industry.

In 1883, the Cherokee Strip Live Stock Association approached Cherokee officials with a proposal to lease the entire Outlet; the Cherokee National Council granted the association a five-year lease for 6 million acres in exchange for $500,000 to be paid in five annual $100,000 payments—much more than the $41,233.81 collected from individual ranchers the previous year. Once the association had secured the lease, it divided the Outlet into 71 individual allotments. Special routes for cattle trails were reserved for the use of all members, and quarantine areas were established. The association levied membership assessments and used the funds to police the range.

In 1885, negotiations for the extension of the original lease began, and the question of who would obtain the lease became a major issue in the 1887 Cherokee tribal elections. Charges of bribery were levied against several tribal officials, and the new chief, Joel B. Mayes, quickly called a special session of the tribal council to settle the issue. Although the Cherokee National Council signed a new lease with the Cherokee Strip Live Stock Association calling for $125,000 per year in rent, Mayes vetoed the bill. Successive bills of $150,000, $165,000, and $175,000 also were vetoed, and, in 1888, Mayes issued a proclamation declaring the original lease was to expire on October 1, 1888. E.M. Hewins, president of the association, hurried to Tahlequah and secured a three-month extension for $43,750, but Mayes repudiated the extension and served notice for the surrender of all property in the Outlet. Finally, in November a new five-year lease was agreed to, calling for an annual payment of $200,000.

Unfortunately for the cattlemen, federal officials maintained that the Cherokees had no right to lease the Outlet and the Jerome Commission began negotiations to purchase it and other tribal lands for $1.25 per acre. Because the cattlemen were willing to pay $3 per acre for the Outlet, the offer was rejected by tribal authorities.

Not to be denied, federal officials decided on a different tactic. On February 17, 1890, President Benjamin Harrison called for the removal of all cattle from the Outlet no later than October 1, 1890. In so doing, federal officials made the land almost worthless to the Cherokees. Three years later, the Cherokees sold the Outlet to the federal government for about $1.40 per acre—$1.60 per acre less than the Cherokee Strip Live Stock Association was willing to pay.

There were other lease arrangements in northwestern Oklahoma. The most famous was the 101 Ranch operation, which was founded by George Washington Miller in 1879 on land leased from the Ponca Indians. Miller's original lease was expanded by his three sons—Joseph, or Joe; Zack; and George—until the 101 Ranch boasted 110,000 acres. By 1905, the ranch was the agricultural showplace of Oklahoma, with an income in excess of $1 million annually. It was also one of the earliest dude ranches in the nation—Easterners, for a fee, spent a brief time on a working ranch with real cowboys. In May 1904, the 101 Ranch hosted 30,000 people for a preview performance of the 101 Round-up Show—the forerunner of the world famous 101 Ranch Wild West Show.

The 101 Ranch was headquartered in the famous White House, near Marland in Noble County. Originally the town was named Bliss, but with the discovery of oil nearby the community's name was changed to Marland in honor of pioneer oilman Ernst W. Marland. Close by is the White Eagle Monument, erected by the Millers in honor of White Eagle, their friend and Ponca chief.

As the range cattle industry ended, wheat became a mainstay of northwestern Oklahoma ranchers and farmers. It is the major cash crop in the state in the second half of the twentieth century, and is second behind cattle and calves in monetary return. Oklahoma's wheat industry received a tremendous boost with the introduction of the hardy winter variety of wheat—Turkey Red—grown as early as 1893 by T.J. Meeker of Blaine County. Later, Joseph Danne of Kingfisher developed a new strain of winter wheat.

Oklahoma continually ranked third or fourth among the nation's wheat producing states. Wheat production is centered in Grant, Garfield, Alfalfa and Kay counties. Oats are grown throughout the region too, with Woodward County ranking first in the state in oat production.

With the acquisition of the Cherokee Outlet, the federal government brought pressure on the Tonkawa and the Pawnee also to accept allotments. There were only about seventy Tonkawa remaining when they signed the agreement in October 1891 assigning 79,276 acres to the public domain. The Pawnees followed a month later and added another 169,320 acres.

President Grover Cleveland issued a proclamation calling for a land run for homesteads in the Cherokee Outlet as well as the Tonkawa and Pawnee reservations. Noon, September 16, 1893, was set for the run. Government land offices were opened at Perry, Enid, Woodward and Alva. To avoid the confusion of the Run of '89, registration booths were maintained, and potential homesteaders issued certificates. The registration booths were swamped. Peddlers sold water for 5¢ a cup to those standing in line to received a certificate.

Fifty-foot-tall Castle Rock in the "badlands" of Woods County. The once prominent landmark for early-day settlers collapsed in 1973, a victim of wind and water erosion.

The registration process was too overwhelming and had to be scrapped.

An estimated 100,000 people took part in the run. The Outlet was divided into K, L, M, N, O and P counties, which correspond to present-day Kay, Grant, Woods, Woodward, Garfield and Noble counties. The Pawnee Reservation was organized as Q County, with Pawnee the seat. Newkirk was named the seat of Kay County, Perry of Noble County, Pond Creek of Grant County, Enid of Garfield County, Alva of Woods County and Woodward of Woodward County.

Woods and Woodward counties initially covered the region west of Grant and Garfield counties; however, at statehood they were divided into five counties—Alfalfa, Major, Woods, Woodward and Harper—

and part of Ellis. Ellis County was formed from the southwestern one-third of old Woodward County and that part of old Grand County north of the Canadian River. Harper County was shaped from the northwestern Woodward County and Major County was formed from the Woods County south of the Cimarron River. In addition, the boundary between Woodward and Woods counties was redrawn along the Cimarron River.

Kay and Noble counties are on the eastern edge of the Cherokee Outlet. The 1893 opening did not include the Kaw and Tonkawa reservations in Kay County or the Ponca and Otoe-Missouri Reservation that covered part of southeastern Kay and adjacent Noble and Pawnee counties. Both the Tonkawa and

Kaw reservations were allotted in 1891 and added to Kay County. In 1904, the Ponca and Otoe-Missouri reservations were allotted and the area divided among Kay, Noble, and Pawnee counties.

The Tonkawa Agency and Methodist School was at Oakland southeast of Tonkawa in Kay County. It was closed in 1910. In 1874, the Kaw Indian Agency was opened at Washunga, west of Ponca City. Washunga is on the banks of the Kaw Reservoir, a 17,000-acre lake on the Arkansas River east of Ponca City. During the Osage oil boom, Kaw City, a major supply point for oilmen, was the home of Laura A. Clubb, the wife of a local oilman. She used her oil money to accumulate a well-known collection of paintings, including Van Marke's *In Pastures*, that were displayed at the Clubb Hotel. Kaw City, once located in Osage County, was covered by the lake and a new Kaw City was built on the western shore in Kay County.

Northwestern Oklahoma had been the center of French fur trading activity 150 years before the Run of '93. Fernandina, in Kay County, had been established by French traders in 1740 as the first non-Indian settlement in the state, with a population of as many as 300 traders, explorers and Indians.

JIM ARGO

Above: *Alabaster Caverns near Freedom. The 200,000,00-year-old cavern is highlighted by glistening, transparent selenite crystals.*
Left: *The terrain of Little Sahara State Recreation Area near Waynoka was created by the almost constant winds from the southwest that formed the sand deposits from the Cimarron River into towering dunes.*

Facing page: *Sunset in the Great Salt Plains. The Great Salt Plains National Wildlife Refuge is a mecca for rock hounds collecting the selenite crystals that are dug from the salt formation.*

The area was also the location of the huge Tonkawa (or Three Sands) Oil Field, discovered by pioneer Oklahoma oilman Ernst W. Marland in June 1921. It was the sixtieth-largest oil discovery made in America in the first half of the twentieth century. Covering only eight square miles, Tonkawa had produced over 124.6 million barrels of oil by 1950. Leases in the pool sold for as much as $2 million per quarter section. It gave rise to the oil boom town of Three Sands. Its main street was the section line separating Noble and Kay counties, and because of its location, it was an easy matter to escape the law officers of either county simply by walking across the street.

Another of Marland's famous wells was the discovery well for the Ponca City Field, the Willie Cries-For-War No. 1. Located on the bank of Bois D'Arc Creek, it was considered sacred land by Ponca who at first refused to allow Marland to drill on the site. However, with the intervention of Joe, Zack and George Miller, Chief White Eagle relented, provided that the well would be located on the slope rather than on the crest. Completed in June of 1911 it marked the first producer west of the Osage. According to legend, Marland was cursed for drilling on sacred land. The oil man later lost his fortune.

Marland's base of operations for Marland Oil Company was at Ponca City, where he established a huge refinery complex. In 1929, Marland Oil was merged with the Continental Oil Company to form Conoco. Marland's palatial home in Ponca City cost $2.5 million and covered 800 acres. In December of 1934 and January of 1935, Marland, who was then governor of Oklahoma, hosted a meeting at his home and laid the foundation for the formation of the Interstate Oil and Gas Compact Commission, which is dedicated to energy conservation. The Pioneer Women statue in Ponca City was designed to represent the pioneering spirit of the women who helped settle the Sooner State. It was a gift from Marland to the people of Oklahoma.

Perry, the seat of Noble County, was founded on the day of the opening of the Cherokee Strip and is the site of the Cherokee Strip Museum. Perry was a wide open frontier settlement that once boasted fourteen saloons and a multitude of gambling houses and brothels in "Hell's Half-Acre" east of the town square. One of the most famous, the Blue Bell Saloon, was operated by Jack Tearney, who sold beer for one dollar a glass to thirsty homesteaders on the day of the Run of '93. Today Perry is the home of the Charles Machine Works, which produces the world-famous Ditch Witch ditch-digging equipment.

In 1908 the county seat of Grant County was moved to Medford from Pond Creek. Many of Medford's early settlers were Mennonites, German speaking farmers attracted by the rich farmland. The *Zions-Bote* or *Messenger of Zion*, a German-language newspaper, was published at Medford for many years. Another center of Mennonite settlement was Deer Creek, east of Medford.

Enid, the seat of Garfield County, was founded because of nearby Government Springs and Skeleton Creek, whose reliable supplies of water made them favorite camping sites on the Chisholm Trail. Selected as one of the locations of the government land offices for the Run of '93, the town was surveyed and platted in 1892. This first survey centered the community around the Chicago, Rock Island and Pacific Railroad depot. But several Cherokees had claimed allotments within the townsite and the location was moved three miles south. The townsite around the depot became known as North Enid and the other as South Enid. Because the railroad wanted to keep the community around its depot, it was not until 1894 that South Enid had rail service. Enid also is the home of Vance Air Force Base, a major facility in the Air Force's pilot training program for both multi-engine and jet-powered aircraft.

The center of one of the nation's major wheat producing regions, Enid's wheat storage facilities were second only to Minneapolis, Minnesota and Kansas City, Missouri. In 1928, Pillsbury Flour opened one of the nation's largest mills in the city. In 1906, the Disciples of Christ founded Phillips University in Enid, and from 1932, the community hosted the annual Tri-State Music Contest featuring high school bands from Oklahoma, Kansas and Texas.

In September of 1914 the Sinclair Oil and Gas Company discovered the rich Garber-Covington Oil Field east of Enid, touching off a major oil boom. The field produced from eleven separate oil horizons and was the nation's primary source of high-grade crude. Production peaked in 1926 with an output of over 10.9 million barrels of oil. Enid was the center of development for the field, and H.H. Champlain, a local banker, was a major developer of the pool. Building on his investment in the Garber-Covington Field, Champlain turned Champlain Refining Company into the world's largest family-owned company engaged in every phase of the petroleum business.

Cherokee is the gateway to the Great Salt Plains and the county seat of Alfalfa County, once ranked as the twentieth largest wheat-growing county in the nation. Near Bryon, natural artesian wells provide water at an average temperature of 60° Fahrenheit for the State Fish Hatchery that opened in 1929.

The seat of Major County was placed at Fairview. The region attracted a number of Mennonite settlers belonging to the Church of God in Christ sect. Meno in eastern Major County is named for their founder, Meno Simons, and is the home of Oklahoma Bible Academy. Deer Creek, Kremlin, Jet, Fairview, Manches-

A salt mine in northwestern Oklahoma during the territorial period. The deposits of salt at the Great Salt Plains, the Little Salt Plains, and along the region's streams and rivers offered a plentiful supply of the mineral that quickly was tapped by pioneers for use as stock salt or for resale.

ter and Orienta are also Mennonite centers. North of Cleo Springs is one of the few remaining original sod houses in the United States.

The seat of Woods County is Alva, the home of Northwestern Oklahoma State University. Southwest of Alva is Waynoka, a major stop on the first transcontinental air route operated by Transcontinental Air Transport, Inc. (TAT), in conjunction with the Pennsylvania and the Atchison, Topeka and Santa Fe railroads. Passengers traveled by train at night and by aircraft during the day. Two Ford Trimotor aircraft were stationed at Waynoka and TAT constructed a $250,000 airport, complete with a two-story hangar at Waynoka, which was the third-largest hangar in the nation when it was completed. Waynona's TAT facility operated until 1930.

Woodward is the seat of Woodward County. One of the community's best-known residents was Temple Houston, the son of Sam Houston and a flamboyant territorial lawyer who became a principal character in Edna Ferber's novel *Cimarron*. In 1947, much of Woodward was destroyed by one of the most powerful tornadoes ever. The twister, almost two miles wide, killed 107 people.

The northwesternmost of the counties created out of the Cherokee Outlet is Harper County, with its seat at Buffalo. Northwest of Buffalo is Doby Springs, homesteaded by Cris C. Doby in 1893. The artesian wells provide an ample supply of water and the location was a well-known camping spot.

Unlike the other sections of Oklahoma, northwestern Oklahoma was settled over several decades by a diverse population—Plains Indians and Southeastern Indians, Texas and Kansas cattlemen, homesteaders from northern states, European immigrants and Eastern oilmen. They gave the region a diverse culture ranging from the Wild West to the urbane East. In addition, its climate fostered a cattle and wheat economy dependent on large land holdings interspersed with small agricultural communities, tied closely to the meatpacking industries of the upper Midwest. Northwestern Oklahoma is a mixture of culture in a state known for its multitude of cultures.

OKLAHOMA GEOLOGICAL CONFIGURATIONS

Name	Location	Description
Arbuckle Hills	northern Carter, western Murray, and southern Garvin counties	low to moderate limestone hills
Arbuckle Plains plains	northern Johnston, southern Pontotoc, and western Murray counties	gently rolling limestone and granite hills and
Ardmore Basin	eastern Carter County	shale and sandstone lowland
Arkansas Hill and Valley Belt	southern Sequoyah, northern LeFlore and Haskell, and eastern Muskogee counties	broad, gently rolling sandstone-capped hills and valleys
Beavers Bend Hills	central McCurtain County	moderate to high hills and ridges
Black Mesa	northwestern Cimarron County	flat-topped remains of a basaltic lava flow from a volacano in Colorado
Boston Mountains	northern Sequoyah, southern Adair, western and southern Cherokee, and eastern Muskogee counties	sandstone capped, deeply dissected plateau
Central Redbed Plains	most of central Oklahoma from Woods, Alfalfa, Grant, and Kay counties on the Kansas border south to Jackson, Tillmon, Cotton, Jefferson, and Love counties on the Red River	gently rolling hills and flat plains formed from red shales and sandstones
Cimarron Gypsum Hills	a thin belt north of Western Sand Dune Belt and Western Sandstone Hills in Canadian, Blaine, Major, Woodward, Harper, and Woods counties	gypsum and shale escarpments and badlands
Claremore Cuesta Plains	most of Muskogee, Wagoner, Rogers, Craig, Nowata, and Washington; eastern Osage; northeastern Okmulgee and McIntosh and northwestern Mayes counties	sandstone and limestone cuestas on broad shale plains
Dissected Coastal Plains	Love, Marshall, Bryan and Choctaw; and southern Johnston, Atoka, Pushmataha, and McCurtain counties	soft sands, gravels, and clay plains
Eastern Sandstone Cuesta Plains	Creek, Okfuskee, Hughes, and Seminole; eastern Osage; western Okmulgee; southeastern Lincoln; northeastern Murray; northwestern Coal and Pittsburg; south and southwestern Haskell and McIntosh counties	sandstone cuestas overlooking broad shale plains
Granite Mtn. Region	southern Kiowa and northwestern Comanche counties	granite mountains
High Plains	Cimarron, Texas, Ellis, and Beaver; western Harper, Woodward, and Roger Mills counties	alluvial sandy, flat uplands, deeply dissected by waterways
Hogback Frontal Belt	northeastern Atoka, southern Pittsburg and Latimer, and central LeFlore counties	sharply dipping sandstone and limestone ridges
Limestone Hills	northeastern Kiowa, southwestern Caddo, north-central Comanche counties	low to moderate limestone hills
Mangum Gypsum Hills	Harmon, southwestern Greer, eastern Greer, and southwestern Beckham counties	gently rolling hills with steep bluffs and badlands formed by gypsum and shales
McAlester Marginal Hills Belt	northern LeFlore and Latimer, central Pittsburg, southeastern Coal, and northwestern Atoka counties	sandstone capped broad hills and mountains overlooking wide, hilly plains
Neosho Lowland	Ottawa, northwestern Delaware, eastern and southern Craig, central Mayes, southeastern Rogers, and north-central Wagoner counties	gently rolling shale lowlands with a few sandstone and limestone escarpments
Northern Limestone Cuesta Plains	eastern Kay and Payne, northeastern Noble and Lincoln, western Creek and Osage counties	limestone cuestas above broad shale plains
Ozark Plateau	Delaware, northern Cherokee and Adair, southeastern Ottawa counties	deeply dissected limestone and chert plateau
Ridge and Valley Belt	northern McCurtain, Pushmataha; southern LeFlore, Latimer and Pittsburg; and northwestern Atoka counties	long sinuous sandstone mountain ridges towering over shale valleys
Weatherford Gypsum Hills	eastern Washita and southeastern Custer counties	gently rolling gypsum hills with many sinkholes and caves
Western Redbed Plains	Washita and Custer, eastern Roger Mills, northern Beckham, and west-central Caddo counties	gently rolling sandstone and shale hills
Western Sand Dune Belts	along the North Fork of the Red River in Tillman, Jackson, Kiowa, Greer, and Beckham counties; along the Canadian River in Blaine and Dewey counties; along the North Canadian River in Oklahoma, Canadian, Blaine, Major, Woodward, and Harper counties; along the Cimarron River in Logan, Kingfisher, Garfield, Major, Alfalfa, and Woods counties; and along the Salt Fork of the Arkansas River in Grant, Alfalfa, and Woods counties	grass-covered alluvium sand dunes
Western Sandstone Hills	northwestern Woods, Custer, and Comanche; eastern Harper; central Woodward; southwestern Major, Blaine, Canadian, and Grady; Dewey; Caddo; southern Washita; northern Stephens and Harmon counties	gently rolling hills formed from soft, flat-lying sandstone cut by steep-walled canyons

INDIANS OF OKLAHOMA

Absentee-Shawnee
Alabama (Alibamu)
Anadarko
Apache of Oklahoma (Kiowa-Apache or Prairie Apache)
Arapaho
Arkansas Cherokees
Apalachicola
Black Bob's Shawnee
Black Pawnee
Caddo
Cahokia
Catawba
Cayuga (Seneca of Sandusky)
Cherokee, (Arkansas Cherokees, Chickamaugas, Eastern Band of Cherokees, Old Settlers, Texas Cherokees, and Western Cherokees)
Cheyenne
Cheyenne-Arapaho
Chickamaugas
Chickasaw
Chippewa
Chiricahua Apache
Choctaw
Christian Indians
Citizen Band of Potawatomi
Comanche
Conestoga
Confederated Peoria
Creek (Muskogee)
Creek Confederacy
Delaware
Delaware of Western Oklahoma
Eastern Apache
Eastern Cherokee
Eastern Shawnee
Eel River
Erie
Euchee
Florida Indians
Fort Sill Apache (Chiricahua Apache, Warm Springs Apache, Wild Apache or Eastern Apache)
Fox
Grand Pawnee
Hainai
Hasinai Confederacy
Hitchiti
Hot Country Ponca
Houechas
Housatonic

Huanchane
Huron
Illinois Confederacy
Inie
Ioni
Iowa
Ilenape
Iroquoian Confederacy
Iswa
Jicarilla Apache
Kadohadocho Confederation
Kansa
Kaskaskia
Kaw (Kansa)
Kichai
Kickapoo (Mexican Kickapoo and Texas Kickapoo)
Kiowa-Apache
Kiowa
Koasati (Quassarte)
Kwahari Comanche
Lipan (Texas Lipan)
Lower Creeks
Mahican Confederacy
Mexcalero Apache
Mexican Kickapoo
Miami
Michigamea
Mingoes
Mixed Shawnee
Modoc
Moingwena (Moins)
Moins
Mohawk
Mississippi Sac and Fox
Missouri
Missouri Sac and Fox
Munsee (Christian Indians)
Muscogee (or Muskogee) (Creek)
Muscogee (or Muskogee) Confederacy
Natchez
Neches
Nez Perce
Northern Comanche
Northern Ponca
Oconee
Ojibway
Old Settler Cherokees
Oneida
Onondaga
Osage
Otoe
Otoe and Missouria

Ottawa
Pawnee
Penateka Comanche
Peoria (Confederated Peoria)
Piankashaw
Ponca
Potawatomi
Potawatomi of the Woods
Prairie Apache
Prairie Potawatomi
Quapaw
Quassarte
Registered Delaware
Sac (Sauk) and Fox
Sauk
Seminole (Florida Indians)
Seneca
Seneca-Cayuga
Seneca of Sandusky
Shawnee
Shawnee of Missouri
Shawnee of Ohio
Skidi
Southern Arapaho
Southern Cheyenne
Southern Comanche
Southern Pawnee
Stockbridge (Housatonic)
Tamaroa
Tawakoni
Tawehash
Tonkawa
Texas Cherokees
Texas Kickapoo
Texas Lipan
Tuscarora
Tuskegee
Uchee
United Peoria and Miami
Upper Creeks
Yamasee
Yuchi
Waco (Honeches, Huanchane, Houechas)
Warm Springs Apache
Western Cherokees
Wea
Wichita (Tawehash)
Wichita and Affiliated Tribes
Wild Apache
Wyandotte
Yuchi (Euchee or Uchee)

CHEROKEE STRIP LIVE STOCK ASSOCIATION LEASEHOLDERS

ANDREWS
BATES AND COMPANY
BEACH AND FAGIN
BEALE
BENNETT AND DUNHAM
BERRY BROTHERS
BLAIR, BATTEN, AND COOPER
BRIDGE, WILSON, AND FOSS
BROWERS
BURRESS
CAMP LYNCH
CAMPBELL
CASTEEN AND MCDANIEL
CATTLE RANCH AND LAND COMPANY
COBB AND HUTTON
COLSON AND MCATEE
COMANCHE POOL
CRAGIN CATTLE COMPANY
CRANE AND LARIMER
CROCKER
CONSTABLE
CORZINE AND GARLAND
DAY BROTHERS
DEAN AND BRODERICK
DICKEY POOL
DOMINION CATTLE COMPANY
DRUMM AND SNYDER
DYE BROTHERS
EAGLE CHIEF POOL GORHAM
ESTES
EWING
FORSYTH
FOSS, BRIDGE, AND WILSON
GOZAD
GREEVER AND HOUGHTON

GREGORY, ELDRED AND COMPANY
HAMMERS, FORBES, AND COMPANYHELM
HEWINS AND TITUS
HOLT
HORSLEY
HOUGHTON
JOHNSON AND HOSMER
KOLLAR AND BROTHERS
MALALEY
MCCLELLAND CATTLE COMPANY
MCCURDY
MICHIGAN CATTLE COMPANY
MILLER
MILLER, PRYORS AND COMPANY
MOORE
NEW YORK CATTLE COMPANY
QUINLAN
RICHMOND
ROBERTS AND SINDSON
S. AND Z. TUTTLE
SCOTT
STEWART AND HODGES
TEXAS LAND AND CATTLE COMPANY
THOMPSON
TOMLIN AND WEBB
TREADWELL
WALNUT GROVE POOL
WALWORTH, WALTON, AND RHODES
WARREN
WICK CORBIN
WICKS
WILEY AND DEAN
WILLIAMSON, BLAIR, AND COMPANY
WORD, BYLER AND COMPANY
WYTHE CATTLE COMPANY

FOR FURTHER READING

Franks, Kenny A., Paul F. Lambert, M.L.Cantrell, Fred S. Standley, and Dee Cordry. *Historic Oklahoma Map Series.* 12 maps, Oklahoma City: Oklahoma Heritage Association, 1990.

Franks, Lambert, and Carl N. Tyson. *Oklahoma Oil: A Photographic History, 1859-1936.* College Station: Texas A & M University Press, 1981.

Franks. *Oklahoma Petroleum Industry.* Norman: University of Oklahoma Press, 1980.

Jackson, Bernice, Jewel Carlisle, and Iris Colwell. *Man and the Oklahoma Panhandle.* North Newton, Kansas: Mennonite Press, 1982.

Litton, Gaston. *History of Oklahoma at the Golden Anniversary of Statehood.* 4 vols., New York: Lewis Historical Publishing Co., 1957.

Morris, John W., ed. *Geography of Oklahoma.* Oklahoma City: Oklahoma Historical Society, 1977.

Morris. *Ghost Towns of Oklahoma.* Norman: University of Oklahoma Press, 1977.

Morris, Charles R. Goins, and Edwin C. McReynolds. *Historical Atlas of Oklahoma.* Norman: University of Oklahoma Press, 1976.

Ruth, Kent. *Oklahoma: A Guide to the Sooner State.* Norman: University of Oklahoma Press, 1957.

Ruth. *Oklahoma Travel Handbook.* Norman: University of Oklahoma Press, 1977.

Skaggs, Jimmy M., ed. *Range and Ranch in Oklahoma.* Oklahoma City: Oklahoma Historical Society, 1978.

Wilson, Steve. *Oklahoma Treasure and Treasure Tales.* Norman: University of Oklahoma Press, 1980.

Wright, Murriel H. *Guide to the Indian Tribes of Oklahoma.* Norman: University of Oklahoma Press, 1951.

Index

Italic numerals indicate photographs

Eagle Pitcher Lead and Zinc Company 40
Eagletown 45, 47
Eakly 86
Earlsboro 51
Eastern Coal Mining District 45
Eastern Sandstone Cuesta Plains 9
Eastern Shawnee tribe 28
Eaton, Marshall Frank "Pistol Pete" 59
Edmond 63
Edmond Sun (newspaper) 63
Eel River tribe 29, 97
El Reno 22, 55–58
Elk Mountain *80*
Ellis County 11, 87, 90, 92, 96
Emory, Col. William H. 83
Empire Oil & Gas Company 36
Enabling Act 62
Enid 92, 94
Erie tribe 28, 97
Ethel Oil Company 32
Euchee tribe 20, 97
Eufaula district 50
Eufaula Reservoir 50
Eureka Gold Mining District 79

Facility (steamboat) 37
Fairview 94–95
Falls Creek 43
Ferguson, Gov. Thomas B. 89
Fern Mountain 40
Fisher, King 58
Five Tribes: and Civil War 21; migration 20; museum 40; named 14–15, *15*; removal of 17–18; territory 48, 53, 79, 89
Flint Creek 41
Foley, Lelia 37
Folsom Bison Hunters 11
Fort Arbuckle 28, 37, 50
Fort Blunt 37
Fort Cobb 83
Fort Coffee 47
Fort Davis 37
Fort Fabry 37
Fort Gibson 37
Fort Gibson Lake *4*, 41
Fort McCulloch 48
Fort Reno *52*, 53, 58
Fort Sill 21, 83
Fort Sill Apache tribe 21, 97
Fort Supply 87
Fort Towson 48
Fort Washita 48, *49*
Foster, Edwin 33
Foster, Henry 33

Foster Petroleum Company 62
Foucart, Joseph 55
Frankhoma Pottery Plant 32
Franklin, Wirt 81
Frazier, Jackson 49
Freedom, town of 87
Frisco 55
Frozen Rock 37

Galbreath, Robert 32
Garber-Covington Oil Field 94
Garfield County 91, 92, 94, 96
Garland, Samuel 48
Garlington 71
Garvin County 28, 50, 86, 96
Gas Processors Association 32
Gate, town of 10, 11, 71
Geary 89
Geronimo 21
Getty, George F. 32
Getty, J. Paul 32
Getty Oil 32
Ghost Dance 89
Glass Mountains *8*, 87
Glenn Pool Oil Field 32
Glover 45
Glover River 43
Goat's Bluff *39*
Goddard, Charles B. 81
Going, William 47
Gold Bell Mining and Milling Company 79
Gold mining 75–78, 79
Goodland 48
Goodwell 71
Gould, Chester 41
Grady County 13, 18, 82, 83, 86, 96
Grand Lake O' the Cherokees 41
Grand River 37
Granite Mountain 96
Granite Mountain Quary *9*
Grant County 88, 91, 92, 96
Grayson 41
Great Salt Plains 9, 87
Great Salt Plains National Wildlife Refuge *92*
Greater Seminole Oil Field 50
Green, D.R. 88
Greenleaf Lake 41
Greer County: geology 75, 96; industry 83–84; mining 79
Greer County Homestead Act 84
Greer, Frank 56, 62

Gregg, Josiah 78
Grove, town 41
Guess, George *26*
Gulf Oil Corporation 32
Gunn, John Noble 67–68
Guthrie 54–55, *56*, *57*
Guthrie, Woody 41
Guymon 71, 74
Gypsum Hills 9, 87

Hainai tribe 82, 97
Hale, William K. 36
Halliburton Services 82
Hallock Park 67
Hammon, Jake 81
Harmon County 75, 84, 86, 96
Harper County 87, 92, 95, 96
Harrison, Pres. Benjamin 54
Hasinai Confederacy 13, 18, 97
Haskell County 37, 96
Haskell, Gov. Charles N. 62
Hatchet, The (newspaper) 55
Healdton Field 80
Heavener Runestone State Park 36, *38*
Hefner, Robert A., Sr. 81–82
Hennessey 59
Henryetta 41
Henryetta Coal Mining District 41, 45
Hewitt Oil Field 80–81
Heydrick, Jesse A. 31
Hickory Creek 80
High Plains 9
Hildebrand Mill 41
Hinton 86
Hitch, James K. 71
Hitchiti tribe 19, 97
Hogback Frontal Belt 96
Hogshooter Natural Gas Field 32
Holdenville 50
Hollis Basin 8–9
Homesteaders: Big Pasture 84–86; cultures 15; in Cherokee Outlet 91–92; in the Wichitas 79; in Unassigned Lands 53–54, 88–89; Mennonites 89; mentioned 14; on Potawatomi land 51; Plains Indians land 30
Hominy, town *26*, 33
Honey Creek *46*
Honey Springs, Battle of 37
Hooker, town of 71
Horseshoe Bend, Battle of 19
Hot Country Ponca 97
Houechas tribe 18, 97
Housatonic tribe 97

Houston, Temple 95
Huanchane tribe 18, 97
Hughes County 37, 96
Hugo, town 48
Huron tribe 97

Ida Glenn No. 1 (oil field) 32
Ilenape tribe 97
Illinois Confederacy 29, 97
Illinois River *39*, 40, 41
Independent Oil and Gas Company 50
Indian Meridian 74
Indian Nations 17
Indian Removal Acts 17
Indian Territory: defined 17; oil discovery 31–32
Indian Territory Colonization Society 53
Indian Territory Illuminating Oil Company (ITIO) 33, 50–51, 62
Ingram No. 1 51
Inie tribe 97
International Petroleum Exposition and Congress 32
Interstate Oil and Gas Compact Commission 94
Ioni tribe 18, 97
Iowa tribe 28, 97
Iron Jacket 90
Iroquoian Confederacy 97
Iswa tribe 97
ITIO 33, 50–51, 62

J.R. Williams (steamboat) 37–40
Jackson County: creation of 84, 85; geology 96; resources 75, 86; towns 83
James, Thomas 37
Janis 48
Jefferson County 96
Jerome Commission 89, 90
Jet, town of 94
Jicarilla Apache 97
Johnston County 8, 49, 96
Jointer City 81
Jones and Plummer Cattle Trail 68
Jones, Robert M. 48

Kadohadocho tribe 18, 97
Kansas, Oklahoma and Gulf Railroad 45
Kaskaskia tribe 28, 29, 97
Kaw Agency 93
Kaw City 25, 93
Kaw Lake 41
Kaw Subagency 25
Kaw tribe 18, 24–25, 92–93, 97